100 Greatest Sports Feats

MAC DAVIS is widely known as a story teller. Readers of his eleven previous sports books number well up in the millions. But many more sports fans have been hearing his fascinating stories broadcast over hundreds of radio and television stations throughout the United States, Canada, and Europe.

He has created and written many of the popular sports shows presented on the air, and hosted by the most famous sportscasters.

In addition, his prolific typewriter has turned out a stream of sports articles for newspapers and magazines, for the interest of teenagers and grownups.

MAC DAVIS

100 Greatest Sports Feats

Grosset & Dunlap · PUBLISHERS · NEW YORK
A NATIONAL GENERAL COMPANY

1972 EDITION

PHOTOGRAPHS USED WITH THE PERMISSION OF
UNITED PRESS INTERNATIONAL, BROWN BROTHERS,
CULVER PICTURES, NATIONAL ENQUIRER,
THE BETTMAN ARCHIVE AND WIDE WORLD PHOTOS
©1964, 1972 MAC DAVIS

LIBRARY OF CONGRESS CATALOGUE NUMBER: 72-75826
ISBN: 0-448-02580-9

PRINTED IN THE UNITED STATES OF AMERICA

TO THE MEMORY OF
JOHN F. KENNEDY
A TRUE FRIEND OF SPORTS.

"The strength of our democracy is no greater than the collective well-being of our people. The vigor of our country is no stronger than the vitality and will of all our countrymen. The level of physical, mental, and spiritual fitness of every American citizen must be our constant concern."

JOHN F. KENNEDY
35th President of the United States

CONTENTS

AN INVITATION

100 Greatest Sports Feats took not only a lot of work, and endless research, but perhaps a lot of nerve, too. For any such selection of an arbitrary number of feats is bound to be controversial.

The history of sports is rich with many unbelievable accomplishments and fantastic exploits. How does one dare choose the greatest 100 feats of all?

To do so, I consulted numerous judges of athletic greatness, and I collected the consensus of the sport historians, the experts, and famous athletes. All graciously have offered me their knowledge, their opinions, and their memories. But the final responsibility for the selection is mine.

Think and say what you will, these 100 feats comprise an awesome panorama of athletic achievement. I'll match them against any accomplishments achieved by mortals in quest of sports glory.

I invite you to a grandstand seat for these epochal performances of athletic greats on their march through sports history.

I hope that sport fans young and old will find this book an adventure in reliving the glories of history's *100 Greatest Sports Feats*.

MAC DAVIS

THE UNCONQUERED INDIAN

IN HIS TIME, the Sac and Fox Indian Jim Thorpe, whose tribal name was "Bright Path," was the most fantastic all-round athlete in sports history. No man ever blazed a brighter path than this magnificent American Indian. A superb performer in many sports, he was exceptionally talented in football, baseball and track. While he was a student at the legendary Carlisle Indian School, he became the greatest college football player of all time. The indestructible Indian played every minute of every game, and he never had a bad day. His exploits on a gridiron were almost beyond belief. All-American Jim Thorpe starred in big league professional football for twenty years.

He was good enough at baseball to make the big leagues and star in the majors for eight years.

However, Jim Thorpe's greatest feat was in track, at the Olympic Games in Stockholm, Sweden, in 1912.

Because he was an athletic genius who could do everything, Jim Thorpe decided to compete in the five-event pentathlon and the ten-event decathlon. This pitted him against the world's best track and field athletes in a grueling test of fifteen different events.

The amazing Indian gave an unbelievable exhibition of all-round athletic skill. He captured the pentathlon by winning the 200 meter dash, the 1,500 meter run, the broad jump, and the discus. He placed third in the javelin throw.

Then he swept the decathlon by winning the shotput, the high hurdles race, the high jump, and the 1,500 meter run. He placed third in the 100 meter dash, the discus, the pole vault, and the broad jump. He finished fourth in the 400 meter race, and the javelin event. In winning both the pentathlon and the decathlon, the fabulous Indian scored twice as many points as did his nearest Olympic rival.

In all Olympic Games history, Jim Thorpe was the only human being versatile enough to win both the pentathlon and decathlon.

So overwhelming were his exploits that King Gustav V of Sweden, the Olympic host, forgot his royal dignity, rushed to Jim Thorpe, clasped his hand in friendship, and shaking with emotion said to the grinning Indian:

"You, sir, are the greatest athlete in the world!"

Historians have agreed. They have acclaimed Jim Thorpe as the greatest football player of all time, and the finest all-round athlete the world has known.

TWICE UPON
A TIME

A NO-HIT NO-RUN game is the supreme accomplishment for a pitcher. In 1875, the first no-hitter was pitched in the major leagues. Since then, of the thousands of hurlers who have pitched for big league fame and fortune, scarcely more than 150 have achieved the rare feat of no-hit pitching perfection. No more than a dozen pitchers in history have had two full-length nine-inning no-hit games during their big-league careers. However, the no-hit feat that Johnny Vander Meer achieved in the 1938 baseball season was the most startling pitching exploit of all.

In 1938, Johnny Vander Meer, a wild south-paw speedster, arrived in the big leagues to pitch for the Cincinnati Reds. The lefthanded rookie started winning from the start, and by June 11 of that season he had scaled the loftiest heights of pitching glory. On that memorable afternoon,

Johnny Vander Meer went to the mound to pitch against the former Boston Braves. At the end of nine innings of play the Braves had no hits and no runs. At twenty-two, Johnny Vander Meer had joined the ranks of no-hit winners.

But "Vandy" had a bigger surprise in store for the baseball world. On June 15, only four days after he had carved his name into the annals of baseball history with his no-hitter, Johnny went to the mound to pitch against the former Brooklyn Dodgers in a night game. A record crowd jammed the Dodgers' ballpark to watch no-hit Johnny in action. All were curious to see if his past feat might have been a fluke. The possibility of a rookie pitching another no-hit game was beyond belief. Up to that time, only seven pitchers in baseball history had been credited with two no-hitters in their careers, and none had achieved his double no-hitters in a single season.

However, early in that June 15 game, Johnny began to awe the crowd with his pitching magic. Inning after inning, he mowed down all the Dodger batters who faced him, without giving up a single hit. A baseball miracle was in the making. A deadly silence fell over the vast crowd, as fans and ballplayers grew tense and nerves stretched taut with the drama. So it was until the crucial last half of the ninth inning, with the score 6 to 0 in favor of Cincinnati. Pitcher Vander Meer was now only three outs away from glory.

With cool confidence Johnny pitched to the first Dodger to face him in the last half of the ninth. He forced him to hit an easy grounder to the infield for the first out. Then, suddenly, the miracle seemed to be vanishing. For Johnny lost control of his speedballs. He walked the next three batters to fill the bases and found himself on the brink of disaster.

Up to bat came Ernie Koy. Vander Meer made him hit an easy grounder to force a runner at home plate for the second out. Then came Leo Durocher, a dangerous hitter in a clutch. He was the last hurdle for Vander Meer. The first pitch was fouled off into the stands. Then "Vandy" hurled his fastest speedball, the batter swung hard, and the ball arched lazily toward deep center field. A Cincinnati player camped under it to make the final putout, completing a baseball miracle. Johnny had done what they had said couldn't be done. He had performed a feat no other pitcher had ever achieved. He had pitched two no-hit no-run games in a row, and he had pitched his back-to-back no-hitters within a period of only five days!

Johnny Vander Meer had achieved the greatest no-hit pitching exploit in recorded baseball history.

THREE CROWNS
FOR LITTLE HENRY

PRIZEFIGHTING with boxing gloves goes back almost one hundred years. Over this stretch of time, hard-hitting men all over the world have fought in roped arenas for fame and fortune; many great fighters have performed memorable feats in boxing. But, on August 17, 1938, one of the most incredible boxing feats of all time was achieved by a dedicated little man who believed that by becoming a boxing champion he would be giving the world an unmistakable sign that he had God's favor and that he had been chosen to speak the word of God. That man was Henry Armstrong.

On that August day he won the lightweight championship of the world. The ring victory completed the most unheard-of record in all boxing history!

No fighter ever began a climb to ring fame and fortune from a more humble beginning than Henry Armstrong. Born in a big city slum, he knew neither parental love nor a happy childhood. Before he was ten, he was a homeless, ragged street urchin, scratching for pennies and begging for food. No one cared whether he lived or died. At thirteen, he was a hardened hobo, wandering aimlessly from town to town, sleeping on park benches or living in hobo jungles. Wherever he went, he was a lonely, half-starved, unwanted boy, scorned by a cruel world not of his making.

His only friends were his two fists: they helped him survive and eventually led him to the prize ring. Little Henry Armstrong became a ring battler before he was eighteen.

Before long, his buzz-saw, whirlwind style of fighting captivated the boxing world. His first glory-day as a prizefighter occurred in October, 1937, when Henry Armstrong fought a title battle against Petey Sarron for the featherweight championship of the world. He won that battle and became the new world's featherweight king.

But the dedicated little man wasn't content to be just the featherweight champion of the world. Armstrong wanted to become a unique champion. He wanted to show the world that he had God's favor so that someday he could speak the word of God and people would listen to him.

Only a few months after winning the featherweight championship, Henry Armstrong went after the world's welterweight crown. He fought the great boxer Barney Ross and emerged from that title battle as the new welterweight champion of the world!

Now Armstrong was a twice crowned ring champion, a rare feat for any fighting man. But he still wasn't content with his fame. He wanted more glory to give the world an unmistakable sign that he had God's favor. So, he went after another boxing title. On August 17, 1938, Henry Armstrong climbed into a ring to battle the world's lightweight champion, Lou Ambers, one of the toughest kings ever to wear that boxing crown. It was a rugged and bloody brawl, but at the end of fifteen brutal rounds little Henry Armstrong's arm was raised in victory, and he became the new lightweight champion of the world!

Within the period of only one year, the amazing Henry Armstrong had won the featherweight, lightweight and welterweight championships of the world. He became the only prizefighter in history to reign over three different boxing divisions as a world champion — at one and the same time!

When Henry Armstrong, the only "triple world champion" in boxing history, finally left the prize ring, he was universally idolized as a boxing immortal. And true to his belief that by winning three world championships he had been chosen to speak the word of God, dedicated Henry Armstrong became an evangelist.

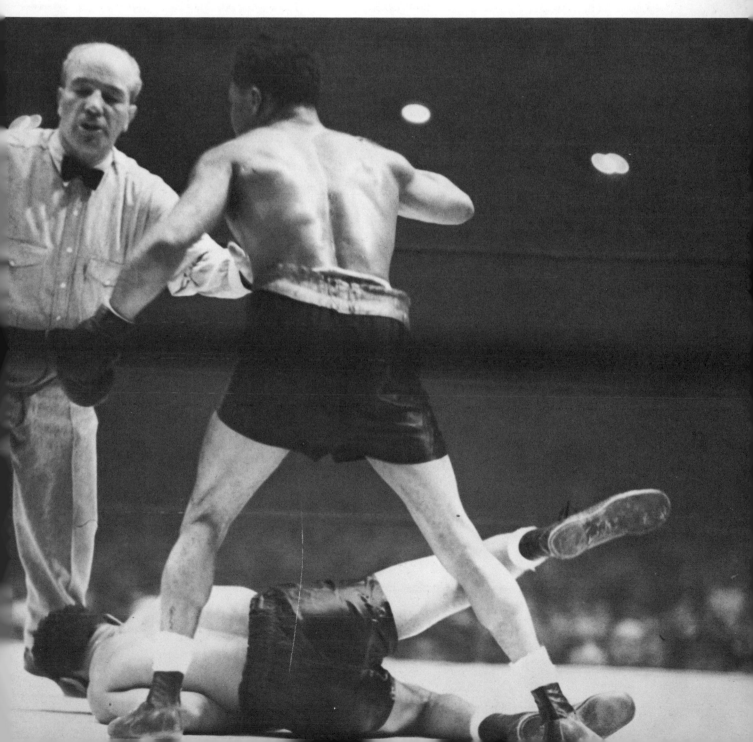

THE DAY THE MONSTERS CONQUERED THE FOOTBALL WORLD

THE TEAM that achieved the ultimate gridiron triumph was the Chicago Bears of 1940. They called them the "Monsters of the Midway." One sunny Sunday afternoon before 36,034 stunned spectators they gave the most fearsome display of power ever seen on any football field.

The Chicago Bears, as winners of the Western Division title in the National Football League, faced the mighty Washington Redskins, the Eastern Division champions, in a game for the world football championship. The cocky Redskins, led by the immortal Sammy Baugh, the greatest forward passer of all time, had no fear of the awesome "Monsters of the Midway." The 'Skins were the favorite choice to win the title playoff game because three weeks before, in a torrid interleague regular-season contest, they had tamed the Bears with a 7-to-3 victory.

The "Monsters of the Midway" were angry when they roared into the nation's capital to play that world championship game; the earlier defeat by the Redskins still rankled. They arrived with a mission — revenge!

The game was less than a minute old when the "Monsters of the Midway" went sixty-eight yards for a touchdown. Moments later, they marched eighty yards for another touchdown. Before the end of the first quarter, they crashed through for a third touchdown. They scored another before the first half ended.

But in the second half, the floodgates opened wider for the rampaging "Monsters of the Midway," and the gridiron massacre became pathetic and almost monotonous. Again and again they rumbled through for touchdowns. Not a single Bear player could do anything wrong. By the end of the third period, the score was 54-to-0, and still the angry Chicago Bears piled it on.

In the final quarter, after the Bears had struck for another touchdown and were lining up for the extra point, the referee pleaded with them:

"Look fellers! Already, you've kicked so many balls into the stands that we now have only one left. How about passing or running for the extra point? Otherwise, we won't have a ball to play with to finish the game."

Ten different players scored eleven touchdowns for the Bears, and six different men scored seven conversions after touchdowns. The team rolled up 372 yards rushing, while holding the bewildered and overwhelmed Redskins to a mere three yards. It was the most one-sided contest in big league pro football history. The final score was an unbelievable 73-to-0.

Not only was it the highest score ever recorded in a world championship football game, but it also was the largest score ever attained by any team in big league professional football history. That feat will ring down through the ages as a monument to the Chicago Bears of 1940 — the greatest team ever assembled to play for the world championship.

IIE WALKED ON AIR

WHEN THE NEW YORK born and raised Bob Beamon came to the University of Texas at El Paso, on an athletic scholarship, his ambition for sports glory was to become a famous basketball player. He stood six-feet-five-inches tall. However, he was persuaded to devote himself to the track team, because he revealed an amazing aptitude for the running broad jump.

Early in 1968, during the indoor track-and-field season, little-known Bob Beamon suddenly blossomed into a super broad jumper, by achieving the most phenomenal long jump ever made indoors. He leaped 27-feet-1-inch and set a new world indoor record. Soon after he shattered this record with a jump of 27-feet-2¾ inches.

Since 1968 was an Olympic year, there was considerable speculation about what lanky Bob Beamon might accomplish in the coming Olympic Games as a long jumper. Later that year Bob Beamon was in Mexico City to compete against the world's greatest running broad jumpers in the Olympic Games. The competitor he feared most was his American teammate, the fabulous Olympic long jump champion Ralph Boston, the first man ever to jump 27 feet, and holder of the Olympic record. Bob Beamon's fear and nervousness were evident when he almost failed to qualify in the preliminary jumps. Twice he fouled in his attempt to reach the final round for the title.

October 18, 1968, a cloudy, dreary and gloomy day, became the most glorious day in Bob Beamon's life. On it he accomplished a feat beyond belief.

Up to that time, the track world believed that a 28-foot long jump was an impossible feat. Bob Beamon not only achieved it, but he made it seem commonplace. On his first long jump in the final round for the Olympic championship, he not only broke the Olympic record by more than twenty inches, becoming the first man in history to achieve a 28-foot broad jump, but at the same time he became the first human being in history to jump 29 feet. His gold medal winning leap through the air measured an unbelivable 29-feet-2½ inches!

This fantastic breakthrough long jump was the greatest individual single achievement in the history of the Olympic Games.

Bob Beamon fell to his knees and kissed the ground when he learned of the miracle he had wrought. He was now the hero of a winning Olympic feat which through the ages will remain the greatest of all miracle long jumps.

A BOY FOR
A MAN'S GLORY

THE YEAR WAS 1913. The event was the United States Open Golf Championship, at Brookline, Massachusetts.

At the time, golf was played almost exclusively by people of means. The greatest player in the world was the legendary Harry Vardon, the symbol of all that is perfect in golf. Second best then, was the fabulous Ted Ray, a magician with a niblick. Those two professionals were the most famous golfers England had ever produced.

In the summer of 1913, with an air of complacent superiority, the two British golf immortals invaded the United States to capture the National Open title. It was a foregone conclusion that either one of them would win America's most coveted golf championship.

Lost among all the famous players who were competing in that tournament, was an unknown amateur from Boston, not yet twenty years old. He was a poor boy from the "wrong side of the tracks" who had learned the game while working as a humble caddie. His name was Francis Ouimet. He was a "million-to-one-shot" to win.

As play began, the weather was foul, and it did not improve as the tournament progressed. Heavy rains had left the course soggy, soft and treacherous. The finest players, one by one, collapsed in a futile attempt to repulse the two British invaders on the march to the championship. But surprisingly, young Ouimet, the green amateur who looked like a choir boy, held his own against the two mighty English professionals as, in a glamorous exhibition of stoicism and skill, he returned blow for blow. After 72 holes of play, Ouimet, Vardon and Ray finished deadlocked for the title, each with a score of 304 strokes.

For Francis Ouimet it was an incredible accomplishment. His epochal feat captured the public's imagination. Overnight, he became a national hero. On September 20, when he went to battle in the 18-hole triple play-off for the 1913 Open championship, the eyes of America and England were focused on him.

It was preposterous to expect further miracles from an amateur player of less than twenty summers in a contest with the two unconquerable professional Goliaths. But Francis Ouimet rose to superb heights, and with shots heard round the world, he repulsed the attack of the British invaders. He not only beat the old master Harry Vardon by 5 strokes, but licked Ted Ray by 6 strokes and became the first amateur in history to win the United States Open Championship.

Ouimet's win stands out as the most stimulating single instance the game has known. His fantastic upset victory revolutionized golf. Overnight, it stripped the game of its stuffy exclusiveness, and golf began to boom in the United States as a popular sport for all.

Francis Ouimet's feat not only made him a golf immortal, but it was the most significant victory ever achieved by a golf player.

KING OF ALL BASEBALL PLAYERS

WITHOUT ANY DOUBT, Tyrus Raymond Cobb was the greatest all-round ball player the world has ever known. Famed in legend as the "Georgia Peach" he was the outstanding phenomenon of big league baseball. He played in more games, made more hits, scored more runs, stole more bases, captured more batting championships, and set more records than any other player in the history of the national pastime. His most unbelievable accomplishment was the fantastic collection of hits he acquired over a period of twenty-four major league seasons.

On the afternoon of August 30, 1905, at Bennett Field in Detroit, gawky eighteen year old Ty Cobb first appeared at bat in a major league game. The Detroit Tigers had bought him for $700. His name was not even on the score card. When the unknown Cobb arrived at the plate for his first time at bat in the majors, he faced the mighty Jack Chesbro, then the greatest pitcher in the game. But the mean-eyed, jut-jawed rookie was unafraid. He twisted his mouth scornfully, braced himself for the pitch, and banged out a double. That hit marked the end of an unknown's journey and the beginning of an epic.

Before that season ended, rookie Cobb made thirty-five more hits. The following season, he collected 112 safe hits. But the year after, he really began to perform as a remarkably versatile hitter; he struck 212 safe blows. As the baseball seasons passed, the colorful "Georgia Peach" con-

tinued to bloom as an incomparable magician with a bat. Eight more times, he collected more than 200 hits in a single season. Ty Cobb was only thirty-four years old when he attained the loftiest heights of batting glory by bagging his 3,000th major league hit. He was the youngest player for that rarest of all batting feats.

However, Ty Cobb was far from done as a magician. Singles, doubles, triples, and homers streamed from his bat in an unending flow. Fourteen times he collected five hits in a single game, and once even six. On July 18, 1927, he performed a feat never before believed possible for a big league batter. He made his 4,000th safe hit—to become the first and only player in history for that feat.

Late in the 1928 season, when Ty Cobb was forty-two years old, during a batting rally, his manager suggested that he give way at home plate for a pinch hitter. The proud "Georgia Peach" angrily snapped back: "Nobody ever hits for Cobb!" He swaggered to the plate, and slammed a safe hit to win the game. He finished that season with a total of 144 hits, and still batting over .300 for his twenty-third consecutive time.

When that major league campaign was over, the aged Ty Cobb quit the big leagues because he had grown bored and weary of hitting baseballs. It completed the most unbelievable hitting saga of all time. He had collected the fantastic total of 4,191 hits.

FOUR MINUTES TO IMMORTALITY

WHEN ROGER BANNISTER was a medical student at Oxford University, he was little known to the track world as a mile runner. However, the science of foot racing fascinated him. He began intensive research work to probe and chart a human being's utmost speed in running a mile distance.

To improve himself as a mile runner, the tall, spare Englishman embarked on a Spartan training program. He drove himself hard, while continuing to carry on his research and experiments in the mechanics of mile running. Using special instruments, he calculated and chartered to the last decimal point just how much oxygen he would need to run the fastest mile in history.

Finally, in 1954, when he was twenty-five years old, this dedicated Briton put aside his scientific charts and research notes and publicly announced that the time had come for him to venture the impossible — to run the first four-minute mile in history.

On May 6, 1954, Bannister came to the Iffley Road track at Oxford University to perform his experiment and prove that the four-minute barrier was vulnerable.

One thousand spectators, mostly Oxford students, watched the blond medical student take his place at the starting line. At his side were two friends, well-known distance runners who had been chosen to pace him in that mile race. But Roger was going to run strictly against the clock.

Guided by his scientific studies and research findings, Bannister ran the first quarter-mile in 57.5 seconds. It was a grueling start. Few in the crowd believed that he would be able to maintain that hard pace. But at the half mile mark he was clocked in one minute, 58.2 seconds. It was even faster than he had planned. At the finish of the third lap, he was clocked in the overall time of 3 minutes and 5 seconds. His exhausted pacers had already faded out. Roger Bannister was now on his own, and there was still one more lap to run. Three hundred yards away from the finish line, Bannister forced himself to run even faster. The crowd went wild at the sight of the game Englishman who, with arms and legs churning, open mouth gasping for air, face twisted by physical strain, sped relentlessly forward. It was a spectacle never to be forgotten. When Roger Bannister flashed across the finish line, the crowd froze into a deadly silence. Breathlessly, everyone awaited the report of the race officials who were busy checking their stop watches. Then came the announcement that was to stun the world. Roger Bannister had done it. The first man in history to break the four minute barrier, he had run a mile in the incredible time of 3 minutes 59.4 seconds.

That run made him a sports immortal.

He was a sports pioneer who achieved one of the most significant athletic feats of all time.

WOMAN AGAINST THE SEA

ON AUGUST 6, 1926, a round-faced nineteen year old American girl, Gertrude 'Trudy' Ederle, was acclaimed by the world for her monumental sports triumph. History recorded it as one of the greatest feminist stories of all time. Her epic feat was a twenty-two mile swim from France to England.

Trudy's heroic swim came fifty-one years after the English Channel was first conquered by a man.

It was 7:09 o'clock on the chilly morning of August 6, 1926 when husky little Trudy, the daughter of a New York City butcher, plunged into the surf at Cape Gris Nez, France to attempt what no other woman had dared before. It was not a favorable day for a watery journey to England. The weather was foul, a strong wind was blowing, and the sullen waters of the English Channel were so choppy and rough that all steamer crossings had been cancelled for that day.

The first few miles went smoothly for Trudy. With her powerful crawl stroke she swam easily and rapidly. The fast pace she set even surprised her trainer aboard the tug following her across the Channel. He cautioned her to slow down, but she splashed on rapidly, determined to cover as much of the watery route as she could before fatigue set in. On and on for hours she swam. By afternoon, after she had been in the water for almost nine hours, the weather and the sea turned so foul and a fierce wind caused such a heavy swell that her trainer became alarmed and called to her to come out of the raging sea and give up the swim. But plucky Trudy refused.

It was 6:30 that evening when she finally swam within sight of the white cliffs of Dover. But a squally rain suddenly came splashing down, making her lonely, heroic struggle against the English Channel even more trying and more dangerous. The spray and the rain lashed her face cruelly, while the mountainous waves buffeted and bounced her around like a toy. It was a miracle that Trudy could keep afloat, much less make any progress under such apalling conditions. No swimmer had ever been subjected to a more brutal test of iron nerve and fierce endurance.

As Trudy finally came within sight of the English shore, thousands of people had already gathered all along the beach to acclaim the amazing American girl. Hundreds of automobiles began blowing their horns, and sirens on the tugs and ships along the English coast joined the

symphony of ear-splitting noise. Hundreds of flares were lit to light her way into port.

It was exactly 9:40 o'clock in the evening of August 6 when Trudy, panting and laughing happily, walked unaided into the shore at Kingsdown — and into the hearts of the world. Not only had she become the first woman ever to conquer the English Channel, but she had performed her monumental achievement in only fourteen hours and thirty-one minutes — the fastest Channel crossing ever achieved by a human being!

The news of her accomplishment electrified the world. Headlines in every language told the story of Gertrude Ederle who, overnight, became one of the most famous women of all time. When she returned to America, nearly two million people lined the streets to welcome her home.

GALLOP OF
AN IRON HORSE

ON THE AFTERNOON of June 2, 1925 veteran Wally Pipp, the regular first baseman for the New York Yankees, complained of a headache before the start of the game. The manager of the team said to him:

"If you're not feeling well, you'd better take the afternoon off. I'll let that big awkward rookie take your place."

No one especially noticed young, eager, broad-beamed Lou Gehrig as he went to play first base for his first time in the majors. Yet, it was a notable occasion. It was not only the beginning of the legend of baseball's indestructible "Iron Horse" but it also marked the start of the greatest consecutive game playing streak of all time!

Fourteen major league seasons, and 5,082 days were to pass before anyone other than Gehrig played first base for the Yankees. The magnitude of Lou Gehrig's endurance in keeping his consecutive playing streak alive, game after game, season after season, was beyond belief. Despite beanings, cracked ribs, chipped bones, broken fingers, muscle tears, pulled ligaments, and tortuous lumbago attacks, Gehrig played on. He made nearly 8,000 appearances at the plate and played in 2,130 consecutive major league games in a row before he finally missed a contest. While compiling the amazing record, Lou Gehrig achieved fame as one of the greatest first-basemen and mightiest sluggers of all time. So unforgettable were his many diamond feats that, eventually, he was enshrined in baseball's Hall of Fame as an immortal. He also helped his team win seven pennants.

On the afternoon of May 2, 1939, minutes before the world champion New York Yankees were about to take the field for a game, captain Lou Gehrig, already a sick man, said to Joe McCarthy, the Yankee manager:

"You'd better put someone else on first base today. I'm taking myself out of the lineup. I'm no help to your ball club anymore."

The manager nodded affirmatively, shrugged his shoulders in despair and simply replied:

"Whatever you think is best, Lou." Quickly he turned away from his famous first baseman, for Lou Gehrig wept, unashamed.

The startling news that the indestructible "Iron Horse" was not going to be on first base after playing in 2,130 consecutive games struck the fans in the ball park like a thunderbolt. It was unbelievable. But before the game was over, the whole baseball world knew of the tragic importance of that day. It would be known in baseball history as the day that marked the finish of the greatest and longest playing streak of all time.

After bowing out that fateful day, the fabled "Iron Horse," Lou Gehrig, never played again Little more than two years later, on the very same June day on which sixteen years before he had begun his great career, Lou Gehrig died of infantile paralysis, at the age of thirty-eight.

However, as long as big league baseball is played, his achievement will be recalled as an endurance record beyond the reach of ordinary men.

THE FLYING DUTCHMAN KEPT HIS PROMISE

ONE DAY in the Thirties, a traveling salesman driving past a farm in California was startled by the sight of a youngster pole vaulting in a spinach patch. Although the farm boy was dressed in overalls, wore heavy shoes and was using a crude homemade pole to propel himself into the air, he was leaping at a height of almost thirteen feet.

The astonished salesman, who happened to be a track fan, lost no time to tell of his discovery to a friend who was a noted college track coach. Eventually, that unknown farm boy was in Fresno State College, pole vaulting for its track team. Thus began the saga of Cornelius Warmerdam, the "Flying Dutchman."

When the Flying Dutchman began to leap beyond fourteen feet, all the track experts concluded that the ultimate height for pole vaulting would be fourteen feet and eleven inches. But Cornelius Warmerdam scoffed at that "scientific" conclusion. He promised to shatter the man-made ceiling for the pole vault event.

On the afternoon of April 2, 1940, in an outdoor track meet at Berkeley, California, the Flying Dutchman astounded the world, becoming the first man in history to pole vault fifteen feet.

Although the track experts now had to recognize that a fifteen foot pole vault jump was possible, they concluded that never would man accomplish a fifteen foot pole vault jump indoors. Again, Cornelius Warmerdam scoffed at the prediction. Again, he promised to shatter a man-made ceiling for the pole vault.

On the night of February 7, 1942 the Flying Dutchman came to New York's famed Madison Square Garden, but he had come to his rendezvous with history handicapped. Along the way,

he had lost his favorite vaulting pole, and he had to borrow another bamboo stick, shorter than his own.

An awesome silence froze the 20,000 spectators shoehorned into the arena as the Flying Dutchman, gripping his borrowed pole, took his place at the end of the long vaulting runway. His moment of truth had come.

Suddenly, he broke into a run, jammed the pole into the slot of the pit, and hurled himself violently toward the ceiling. He scissored and twisted his body while his legs kicked for space over the crossbar. In the twinkling of a second his leap was over, and he plummeted down into the pit. The crowd went wild with frenzied joy. The Flying Dutchman had cleared 15 feet, ⅜ inches to become the first man ever to achieve a fifteen foot pole vault jump indoors.

By becoming the first athlete in history to shatter a man-made "ceiling" for a track event, Cornelius Warmerdam proved that barriers are made to be broken.

THE FIGHTER WHO COULDN'T LOSE

WHEN ROCCO MARCHEGIANO, son of an Italian immigrant shoemaker, was a teenager in Brockton, Massachusetts, his life's ambition was to become a big league baseball player. When the day finally came that a major league club gave him a tryout, young Marchegiano was a dismal failure: he was too clumsy and lacked finesse as a diamond catcher. Changing his name to Rocky Marciano, he used his enormous strength and hard fists to become a prizefighter.

As a professional boxer, Rocky was a parody on the great heavyweights who had preceded him. He was awkward, crude, clumsy. Futhermore, he possessed no knowledge of the art of boxing. All Rocky could do inside a ring was punch.

But how he could do that! He bowled over a string of opponents, mostly by knockouts, until eventually the "Brockton Blockbuster," as he was nicknamed, muscled himself into contention as the worthiest challenger for the world's heavyweight boxing title.

On September 24, 1952 in Philadelphia's vast municipal Stadium, before a crowd of over 50,000 ring fans, Rocky Marciano found himself facing the aging but cagily ring-wise world's heavyweight champion, Jersey Joe Walcott, in a battle for boxing's richest, most coveted crown.

In the initial round of that championship battle, Rocky was knocked down for the first time in his life. After the count, he rose to his feet humiliated but determined. For twelve torrid rounds he continued to absorb a cruel beating from the fists of the foxy champion. Then in the thirteenth round, Rocky fired one of his blockbuster blows that traveled no more than six inches before it caught the champion on his chin. It was one of the hardest punches ever seen in a heavyweight title fight. The stunned champion crumpled to the canvas, to be counted out. With surprising suddenness, Rocky Marciano, whose clumsy ability as a fighter had been deprecated and ridiculed, became the new heavyweight champion of the world.

In the years that followed, champion Rocky Marciano took on all comers in defense of his title and he never lost! His awesome punching power became a national byword. In 1956, Rocky retired from the ring while still the undefeated heavyweight champion of the world. Only when he had left the ring was the true significance of his great feat fully understood and appreciated. From his first fight to his last as a professional pugilist, he had never lost a ring bout. His boxing career that had begun in obscurity ended in world fame and fortune. Rocky Marciano had fought in the ring forty-nine times, and had won forty-nine straight victories — forty-three by knockouts! His record may remain unmatched for all time.

A CYCLONE
IN THE BALLPARK

DENTON TECUMSEH YOUNG came off a mowing machine on an Ohio farm to pitch in professional baseball. On August 6, 1890 when he was twenty-three, he appeared in his first major league game. The ball park rocked with laughter at first sight of the hayseed who had been outfitted hurriedly with a patched-up, crazy-quilt baseball uniform too small for him, standing at six-foot-two and weighing 210 pounds. Despite his harlequin garb and the ridicule, the big farmer made a triumphal major league debut. He pitched a three-hit victory for the Cleveland club against the Chicago White Stockings. No one ever again laughed at the "rube" who because of his blinding speed quickly earned the nickname of "Cyclone."

Thus, Cy Young began the most incredible victory saga ever created by a major league pitcher. Before the season ended, he won eight more games.

In his first full season as a big league pitcher, Cy Young wasted no time in amazing the baseball world with his pitching magic. He won twenty-seven games. The following season he went further; he won thirty-six games. The season after that he won thirty-two.

As the seasons went by, the tireless right-hander became the most wondrous pitcher in the history of major league baseball. He bagged more winning seasons than any other hurler known to the game. Fourteen times in a row Cy Young won twenty or more games a season. Five times in a row, he won thirty or more games a season. In his twenty-two seasons in the majors, he pitched 906 games. No other hurler ever participated in as many big league contests.

On a blistering hot afternoon in the 1911 season, when Cy Young was forty-four, he went to the mound to hurl a game for the Boston Nationals. In an unforgettable 12-inning pitching duel, against a sensational young hurler half his age, old Cy Young lost that game by a score of 1-to-0. He never pitched another major league game. Although his arm was as good as ever, he decided to call it a career. He quit the majors not because he had grown too old, but because he was disgusted with himself, for he had grown too fat to field bunts.

It ended the most unbelievable long-span winning feat ever achieved by a big league pitcher. In the twenty-two seasons he twirled on the mound, he won a fantastic total of 511 games!

As long as baseball will be played, that record will continue to glorify Denton Tecumseh Young as the winningest pitcher of all time.

THE IMPOSSIBLE BOAT RIDE

THE AFTERNOON of the twenty-third of July, in 1955, the sky was heavy and ominous with clouds, and the seven-mile stretch of treacherous water in the Cumbrian Mountains, known as Ullswater, looked black and forbidding. However, England's famous daredevil, Donald Campbell was there with his "Bluebird" to keep a rendezvous. Bluebird was a turbo-jet hydroplane speedboat, and it was Campbell's dream to pilot his beautiful craft at the unbelievable speed of 200 miles an hour.

"Man can never do it" had said the world. Other daredevils before him had attempted to break the "water-barrier" by driving speedboats at 200 miles an hour, but all had died violently when their crafts blew up and disintegrated at that impossible speed.

When Donald Campbell entered the silvery cockpit of Bluebird, he was grumpy and depressed. A vertebrae in his spine was out of place, and stabbing pains in his back tortured him. But this was the day he had chosen for his sail to fame, and everything was now ready for his brave adventure against the gods of fate.

He gunned his speedboat, and Bluebird, the most powerful craft ever built, rocketed forward. It zoomed to 100 miles an hour, on to 150, and then it passed the world's speed record of 178.497 miles an hour. Donald Campbell pushed Bluebird to even greater speed.

When he entered upon the measured kilometer course, "the impossible" happened. He broke the "water-barrier," as his Bluebird thundered over the water at 202.32 miles an hour.

When that historic ride was over, even the ice-blooded Donald Campbell had tears in his eyes. He had lived through the most memorable day of his life.

In 1959, the man who shattered the "water-barrier" performed an even more incredible feat with a speedboat. In a test on Coninston Water in England, Donald Campbell drove a craft at an unbelievable speed of 275 miles an hour and lived to tell the story.

THE FIRST
OLYMPIC MARVEL

ALVIN C. KRAENZLEIN was the track wonder of his time. When only a nineteen-year-old student at the University of Pennsylvania, already he had set several intercollegiate, national, and world records.

However, in 1900, at the Olympic Games in Paris the lanky American youngster reached the zenith of his fame. There he achieved a feat that stands alone in Olympic glory.

Although, he was pitted against the world's greatest track performers of his day, he won the 60-meter sprint, the 110-meter high hurdles, the 200-meter low hurdles, and the running broad jump. Unbelievable as was his achievement in winning four individual Olympic track championships, even more incredible was the manner of his triumphs. For in winning each event, he set an Olympic record.

In all the history of the Olympic Games, only Alvin Kraenzlein ever achieved the impossible feat of winning four individual championships in one set of Olympic Games.

ONLY
THE JONES BOY
DID IT

PRIOR TO 1930, the sunset year of the fabulous era known as the Golden Age of Sports, for a man to achieve "The Grand Slam" in the ancient game of golf was unthinkable. But in 1930, Bobby Jones accomplished that feat to go down in history as the greatest golf immortal of all.

Bobby Jones was an unlikely candidate for the golfing crown. Born a weakling, he was a sickly boy suffering most of the time from stomach disorders. Although he began to play golf at a tender age, his chances to become a golf-great were remote. He was hot-tempered, impatient to learn and given to wild tantrums when things went wrong. Before he was seventeen, Bobby had become so bitterly disappointed with his golf

game that he wanted to quit playing forever. But he was persuaded to continue, and learned to discipline his fiery temper. By the time he was twenty-one, he had captured thirteen major golf championships on two continents and had won almost every important title known to golf. A true amateur who played golf only for the sport of it, he was the favorite in every tournament he played, regardless of place or competition. Throughout the golf world he was acclaimed the most skilled shot-maker of all.

Early in 1930, Bobby journeyed to Scotland to play in the British Amateur Championship. It had been the one coveted national golf title to elude him. The 1930 British Amateur tournament was played on the famed wind-swept St. Andrews course — the birthplace of golf. Bobby raced through that tough tournament and won it with an amazing exhibition of precision shotmaking that stunned the spectators.

He returned to America to a wild and tumultuous homecoming welcome. Almost a million people lined the streets of New York for a ticker-tape parade to pay tribute to him.

Then Bobby Jones went to Minneapolis to play in the famed United States Open Championship at Interlachen. Although he was tired and weary from the strain of winning England's two major championships, once again he faced the world's greatest golfers in a grueling contest. That summer, the heat in Minneapolis was unbearable, and with all eyes on him every minute of play, Bobby was under terrific pressure. Never before had a golfer captured the British Open and the United States Open in the same year. But Bobby Jones did it.

With three of golfdom's most coveted championships safely tucked away, Bobby Jones now proceeded to Ardmore, Pennsylvania and the Merion Cricket Club where the United States Amateur Championship tournament was to be staged. The sports world speculated on Jones' chances to accomplish the impossible — win all four of golf's most coveted national championships in a single year. It was a task for a superman. At Ardmore, Bobby Jones proved himself just that as he crushed every opponent in his way to win the U.S. Amateur title. His final golf triumph in 1930 made him the first and only player in history to score the "Grand Slam" of golfdom by winning the British Amateur, the British Open and the United States Amateur and Open Tournament in the same year!

Bobby Jones, who had captured the U.S. Amateur title five times, the U.S. Open championship four times, the British Open three times, and the British Amateur once, found himself with no more golf worlds to conquer. The "Grand Slam" had capped his fabulous career. In November, 1930, he retired from competitive golf at the age of twenty-eight, a strange finish to the saga of a peerless golf champion.

A LEMON TURNED
INTO A PEACH

WHEN NINETEEN-YEAR-OLD Richard "Rube" Marquard came to the big leagues in 1908 to pitch for the New York Giants, his arrival created a sensation. The Giants had bought him for $11,000, an enormous expenditure for a major-league player in that time. When the wrynecked southpaw won only nine games in his first three seasons as a big leaguer, a mocking baseball world dubbed him, "the $11,000 Lemon."

However, in 1912, the angular left-hander shook off his odious nickname by performing a winning feat unique in modern major-league history.

On the afternoon of April 11, Rube Marquard pitched the Opening Day game of the 1912 season. He won it by a lopsided score. Five days

later, again he went to the mound to pitch, and again he won with ease. As that pennant campaign went on, the stylish Rube pitched against every team in the National League and he always won. By the end of May, he had reeled off ten victories in a row.

As he continued to pitch and win, Rube Marquard became the wonder of the baseball world. With every game, the tension grew greater for him as he continued to add triumphs to his amazing winning streak. It was a terrific strain to win his fourteenth game in a row—an eleven inning pitchers' battle.

Then he won his fifteenth straight victory, on to his sixteenth and seventeenth, and then his eighteenth in succession. The tension became almost unbearable for the slim southpaw. On the nights before he had to pitch, Rube could neither eat nor sleep. On July 3, when he won his nineteenth game in a row, he was wildly acclaimed as a wonder of the age.

On July 8, Rube faced the Chicago Cubs. He was driven from the mound, and finally, he suffered his first defeat of that season. It ended the longest winning streak ever achieved by a modern major-league pitcher.

Richard 'Rube" Marquard hurled in the majors for nineteen years. He won more than 200 games, and sparked five teams to pennants. But his greatest fame as a pitcher was his winning streak of nineteen straight victories.

A SHOEMAKER
AT HIS TRADE

No JOCKEY ever made a faster ride to turf fame than Willie Shoemaker. The fifty-eight inch Texan was only seventeen when he rode his first winner. But before he was thirty, he had become the first jockey in history to capture the national riding championship five times, the first to win two-million dollars in racing purses in a single year, and the first to boot home more than 4,000 winners in only a dozen years of racing. Grown into a turf legend before his thirtieth birthday, Wee Willie "The Shoe" became the youngest jockey ever to be enshrined in racing's Hall of Fame.

The first great feat of his incomparable career as the most fabulous of all winning jockeys was achieved in 1935: he was the first rider in turf history to boot home 400 winners in a year. He rode 485. But his greatest feat as the winningest jockey of all-time happened in 1971 when he piloted to victory — winner number 6,033.

SIXTY-ONE BLOWS
FOR MARIS

GROWING UP IN the obscurity of the western hills and plains, Roger Maris was a flashy school-boy hero at Bishop Stanley High in Fargo, North Dakota. Although he starred in football, basketball and track, he had little interest in baseball because his school had no baseball team.

At that time, if some soothsayer had told people that this quiet and reticent country boy would gain imperishable fame as a big league baseball hero by eclipsing the feats of the greatest home run sluggers of all time, he would have been called stark mad. Yet, Roger Maris was destined to make headlines.

Roger was only nineteen years old when he turned to professional baseball. For five years he drifted around in the obscurity of the minors before his diamond talents were recognized by a major league club. In his first four seasons in the big leagues, outfielder Roger Maris played for three different teams. Everywhere he played he was just another face in the crowd. Not even once did he attain a .300 batting average. However, during his first four years in the majors, he managed to belt ninety-seven homers.

When the 1961 baseball season started, no one in his right mind expected the New York Yankee right-fielder to launch an assault on the home run record of sixty which the immortal Babe Ruth had set thirty-four years before. That mark was a matchless symbol of baseball power and a legend for the ages.

As that season progressed, Roger Maris grew quite despondent. His timing was off and his graceful swing was producing few homers. At the end of May, he was batting a precarious .248, and he had hit only twelve four-baggers. By the end of June, he had clouted twenty-seven, by July's end he had socked forty, and by the end of August, he had slugged fifty-one home runs.

Now the eyes of the whole sports world were upon him. Suddenly, Roger Maris found himself to be a hero. His privacy was torn to shreds, and he became bewildered by the ever-mounting pressure building around him as baseball's newest home run idol. He nearly cracked under the strain.

On September 26, Roger Maris hit his six-tieth home run of the season. But his assault on the homer record was not yet complete. The finish came on Sunday, October 1, the last day of the 1961 baseball season. The New York

Yankees were playing the Boston Red Sox. Tracy Stallard, a fastball right-hander was the rival pitcher. More than 25,000 curious fans huddled in the vast Yankee Stadium to witness Roger Maris' final bid for grandeur.

In his first time at bat, Roger flied out. In the fourth inning he came to bat for the second time. The clock on the huge scoreboard read 2:42 and there was no score, one out, and no one on base. The pitcher fired a fastball high and outside. The umpire called it a ball, and an angry rumble of boos mocked the cautious hurler. Stallard threw another fastball, low and inside, and again the ump called it a ball. The booing from the stands grew louder.

With the count two balls and no strikes, Maris hitched up his trousers, knocked the dirt out of his spikes, and ominiously pumped his bat. He wanted no free walk to base, only a chance to hit the ball. The next pitch came, a fastball knee-high on the outside corner of the plate. Maris swung and the white baseball soared through the sunshine, sailing more than 360 feet from the home plate into the right field stands. As Roger Maris slowly circled the bases to complete his historic four-bagger, a wild ovation acclaimed him a new diamond immortal. When he tried to retreat into the dugout, his delirious teammates pushed him back into view, again and again, to wave his cap at the roaring crowd.

THE TALL MAN OF TENNIS

THE BEGINNING OF William Tatem Tilden as a tennis player was ludicrous. In his youthful years, he was a hopeless failure on the courts. He rarely won a tennis match. However, he practiced constantly and with such tireless fervor and grim determination that the tennis world mocked him as a nut.

Lanky Bill was twenty-seven when he began to blossom out as a tennis great. Before long he was in a class by himself. A matchless master of every tennis stroke, he became the most colorful, the most famous, and probably the greatest player in the history of tennis. He dominated the sport longer than any other player.

For ten years in a row, from 1920 through 1929, he was the top ranking amateur in the world. He played on the American Davis Cup team for eleven years, and only he in Davis Cup history ever won thirteen challenge singles matches in a row. As an international Cup competitor, he accomplished a feat beyond compare. For he lost only once, in doubles, in a total of twenty-two Davis Cup matches.

During his fabulous reign as the world's tennis champion, Tilden had an accident. The middle finger of his right hand was amputated. A shocked sports world believed that Big Bill, with only four fingers on his playing hand, was finished as a tennis champion. But he surprised everyone by coming back to the tennis wars and going on to even greater glory as a tennis champion who had no equal.

He was the first American to win the men's singles championship of Great Britain. He captured the famed Wimbledon title two more times.

Roaming all over the civilized world to duel with the greatest tennis players of many nations, he won more than one-hundred major tennis titles. His long legs carried him into tennis battle in over ten thousand matches, and for almost two decades he was invincible.

Millions of people idolized him as a hero. Kings, royalty, statesmen, and most of the world celebrities of his time fawned upon him.

His career was so spectacular that it is impossible to single out his greatest accomplishment. But perhaps his outstanding achievement was winning the United States Singles Championship seven times!

Tilden's longevity as a tennis great bordered on the unbelievable. As an amateur and a professional, he competed against the world's greatest players and still continued to win until he was fifty-three years old.

The sports world never had so incredible a tennis champion as William Tatem Tilden, and may never have his like again.

THE GREAT ROBBERY

THE GREATEST series of thefts in baseball history took place in 1962. They were committed by a slightly-built, sad-faced, religious little man of thirty, the son of a minister. He was Maury Wills, a shortstop for the Los Angeles Dodgers. For years he had knocked around baseball as an obscure and unwanted ball player, because he was too small and too frail. But during the 1962 major league season, that artful Dodger boldly stole so many bases that he became known as the greatest "diamond burglar" in modern baseball history.

It was on April 13 of that big league pennant campaign when Maury Wills stole his first base of the season. By April's end he had stolen eight bases. But few seemed to care, and his larceny intimidated no one. By the end of May, the swifty shortstop had swiped twenty-seven bases; forty-two by the end of June, and fifty-two before July had run out.

Suddenly, the baseball world, ever in search of new gods to worship, recognized Maury Wills as a diamond hero beyond compare. It acclaimed him with uninhibited delight. "Go-go-go Maury!" became a familiar cry in big league ballparks.

By the end of August Wills had stolen seventy-three bases. His tiny body was so battered and bruised from his daring larceny that often he was forced to resort to the "belly slide" in order to continue his assault on the all-time stolen base record of ninety-six which had stood unchallenged for forty-seven years. It was one ancient baseball record they said "couldn't be broken!"

But Maury Wills with the twinkling legs and larceny in his heart was not to be denied. In September his pilfering of bases became almost unbelievable. On September 23, in the 156th game of that season, he matched the ancient all-time record by stealing his ninety-sixth base. Before that game was over, he had surpassed the unsurpassable by stealing another.

However, the daring Maury Wills went even further. By the end of that season he had stolen 104 bases!

His bold and fantastic achievement was the greatest feat of base stealing in modern baseball history.

THIS IS THE WAY IT HAPPENED

On July 26, 1908, in London, seventy-five of the world's greatest long distance runners lined up before King Edward VII of Great Britain and Queen Alexandria for the start of the Olympic marathon race. Among those great runners was an apple-cheeked seventeen-year-old American boy named Johnny Hayes. Back home, he had been an obscure department store ribbon clerk. But on that summer day in England, he was the "baby" of the United States Olympic team.

Johnny Hayes never before had run a marathon race and had been tossed into the grueling 26-mile, 385-yard Olympic foot race purely for practice. The favorite to win that marathon was Italy's incomparable Pietri Dorando, then the world's greatest long distance runner.

No sooner had the Olympic event started than Dorando the Great raced into the lead, holding it easily as he churned off the miles. The day was hot and fiercely humid, and the weather took its inexorable toll of runners. When Dorando came running into Shepherds Bush Stadium where 100,000 spectators waited to see the finish of the Olympic marathon race, he appeared to be a certain winner. But the Italian showed signs of his ordeal: when he was scarcely more than one hundred yards from the finish line, Dorando began to stagger. Suddenly, he collapsed on the track. There were sympathetic cries of "Give him a hand up!" followed by warning shouts of, "Nobody touch him! It's against the rules!"

As Dorando lay helpless on the ground, the finish line within sight, into the stadium came Johnny Hayes, legging it toward the finish line with ease and power. At the sight of the American runner, panic seized some of the muddled British Olympic officials who rushed out on the track, picked up the fallen Italian runner and half-carried, half-dragged him across the finish line, only a few steps ahead of Johnny Hayes who completed that marathon race under his own power. The confused and wild finish became the most dramatic single episode in Olympic history!

When it was first officially announced that Dorando was the winner of the marathon there was such a hue and cry that it almost created an international incident. But three hours after the finish of the controversial race, Johnny Hayes was properly and officially proclaimed the winner of the 1908 Olympic marathon!

That victorious race catapulted the slim, seventeen-year-old boy to world fame. When he returned home, nearly a million people lined the streets to give him a hero's welcome! Only Johnny Hayes ever won a marathon race in the Olympic Games for the United States.

THE STRANGLER

WHEN ROBERT FREDERICKS quit playing semi-pro baseball to wrestle professionally, all he knew about the ancient sport of wrestling was what he had learned from a fifty-cent mail-order instruction book written by a man named Evan Lewis. In tribute to his wrestling teacher, whom he had never seen in person, the nineteen year old American youngster billed himself as Ed Lewis.

Before long, because of the lethal headlock he had perfected and used to win his wrestling matches, he became famed and feared throughout the world as Strangler Lewis.

In the Roaring Twenties, the Golden Age of Sports, Strangler Lewis not only reigned as the heavyweight wrestling champion of the world, but also was acclaimed the greatest catch-as-catch-can grappler of all time.

The tireless Strangler continued to wrestle professionally until he was forty-three years old. No other wrestler engaged in as many pro mat contests. He took on all contenders for 6,200 wrestling bouts. He alone earned from wrestling a fortune of five million dollars, and he alone captured the world's heavyweight wrestling championship five times.

BASKETBALL'S AMAZING NOBODIES

THEY SAID it couldn't be done. No college basketball team had ever won both the National Invitation Tournament and the NCAA Tournament in the same season, and the youngsters who played for the City College of New York were a most unlikely group to break such a precedent.

CCNY was not a school noted for the prowess of its athletic teams. It was an egghead school that made no special allowances for boys with supple muscles and superior reflexes. Nevertheless, though City was not a national powerhouse, Coach Nat Holman's basketball teams had always turned in respectable records.

But the members of the 1949-50 team were a special breed. Take Ed Warner, only a sophomore, but at 6-2 a human jumping jack with astounding body control. Irwin Dambrot, 6-4, an aggressive rebounder, a good ballhandler, and Norm Mager, the cool opportunist, were seniors. Completing CCNY's impressive line-up were sophomores Ed Roman, the center with the soft pop shot from outside, Floyd Layne, always on the move, driving, and Al Roth, steady and strong, with a fine outside set shot.

CCNY was the final and ostensibly the weakest entry in famed Madison Square Garden's NIT. The team's regular season record of 17-5 was good enough, but hardly the sort that would scare the opposition. No one gave them a chance.

But the Beavers had come to play. When they thrashed defending champion San Francisco, 65-46 in the opening game, no one was excited. Kentucky, with its seven-foot center, Billy Spivey, would put them in their place. The score of that match was CCNY 89, Kentucky 50—and, at last people began to take notice of the "Cinderella" team. Next it was Duquesne that succumbed, 62-52. In the tourney final, Bradley was heavily favored to win. Yet when the action was over CCNY was the NIT champion by 69-61. The Beavers were immediately tapped to fill out the field for the NCAA tournament.

Coach Holman was optimistic about his team's chances. That drew a laugh from the experts. Better, more consistent teams than City had tried to win both post-season shows without success. But Nat Holman's charges refused to believe that it couldn't be done. They played their game, squeaking past Ohio State, 56-55; then they beat North Carolina State, 78-73. Once again they faced Bradley in the tournament finals. It was a game to fire the imagination—the hard-driving underdogs against a Bradley team sparked by All-Americans Paul Unruh and Gene Melchiorre and determined to avenge their NIT defeat.

The dream game was played in Madison Square Garden before a sellout crowd. Bradley started out with a surprise—a zone defense. But City took it in stride, and at halftime it was CCNY 39, Bradley 32. The crowd anticipated a Bradley comeback in the second half, but City carried its lead into the last minute of play. It was 69-64 when, with electrifying quickness, Melchiorre, the 5-8 Bradley speedster, scored a pair of driving buckets. City led by one point with 42 seconds left!

It was City's ball but, suddenly, there was Melchiorre again, hawking aggressively. He snatched up a loose ball and drove hard toward the basket. It seemed like a certain hit. Yet even as he went up for the shot, Irwin Dambrot was stealing the ball from his fingertips. Dambrot let loose a long downcourt pass to teammate Mager, who cut toward the Bradley foul line. Mager layed it in, and the game was over. City College had won, 71-68!

They said no one could win both of these tournaments in a single college basketball season. But the kids from the sidewalks of New York—the CCNY wonder-five—did it!

HE OUTWALKED
THEM ALL

As a long distance walker an American named Edward Payson Weston had no parallel.

In 1867, after he had first tested himself by a 478 mile walk which he made in less than ten days, twenty-eight year old Edward Payson Weston made a wager of $10,000 that he could walk from Portland, Maine to Chicago, Illinois — a distance of 1,326 miles — in twenty-six days. Six judges and a flock of reporters, all riding in horse-drawn carriages, accompanied him on his walk. Weston walked that distance in two hours less than the time called for and became America's first celebrated sports hero!

His fame as a walking champion soon spread throughout the world. He traveled all over the globe, walking against the best of every land. He always won.

In 1876, he went to England to walk against Great Britain's mighty champion, Perkins. They met in a twenty-four hour walking race for a $25,000 purse. After sixteen grueling hours of walking, the Englishman quit, but Weston walked on to the end, to win the race.

For many years, no one in the world could outwalk Edward Payson Weston, as he performed incredible tests of endurance. Once, he walked 5,000 miles in one hundred days. In 1909, he walked from New York to California — a distance of 3,895 miles in one hundred and four days. Then, to show that he was still the hardiest and fastest walker in the world, as well as the greatest in history, he turned right around and walked back another 3,600 miles in only seventy-seven days.

That round trip transcontinental trek was the greatest walking feat ever achieved by a man. When Edward Payson Weston completed his final long distance walk of 7,495 miles, he was seventy years old.

FIFTY-SIX
FOR JOLTING JOE

THROUGHOUT the long history of big league baseball, many great players have achieved unusual hitting feats. But the most incredible streak of consecutive safe hitting of all time was achieved by Joe DiMaggio. No one has since come close to his record nor is it likely anyone ever will.

In the fourteen seasons Joe DiMaggio was an outfielder for the New York Yankees, he gained lasting recognition not only for being the most graceful centerfielder of all time and the first player in history to be paid a season's salary of $100,000, but also because he was such a fine all-round ballplayer. Eventually he was enshrined in baseball's Hall of Fame. However, the greatest feat of his fabulous major league career was the hitting streak which he ripped off in the summer of 1941.

There was no warning that something was on the way that May 15 afternoon when in a losing game against the Chicago White Sox Joe DiMaggio rapped out one safe hit in four times at bat. It was routine hitting for the great "Jolting Joe" who in two previous seasons had won the American League batting championship. There was no excitement when he hit safely in the next few games. DiMaggio's hitting streak sputtered along for more than two dozen consecutive games before anybody was aware of it. But when it climbed to thirty consecutive games the entire baseball world suddenly became excited. Jolting Joe continued to hit in game after game, holding an entire nation in his grip with a magnetic force no one imagined a ballplayer could exert.

As Jolting Joe continued to hit safely and carried his streak past the milestones erected by baseball's greatest hitters, everybody began to wonder when and if ever he would be stopped. The relentless day-by-day pressure was terrific, more than any other big league player ever had to face. The pitchers he faced in game after game now bore down more than ever. Every hurler wanted to be the man to stop the Yankee Clipper. Even the rival fielders now were more on their toes when Joe DiMaggio came to bat. They tried

many spectacular catches to rob DiMaggio of sure hits. But in game after game Jolting Joe continued to collect safe hits.

His fabulous streak stretched to fifty and still surged upward. DiMaggio wasn't finished. On July 16, he rapped out three hits in a game against the Cleveland Indians to make it fifty-six games in a row!

The next day, almost 70,000 fans stormed into the Cleveland ballpark to see DiMaggio add one more game to his hitting streak. But for that one game, Joe's hot bat was finally cooled off and ran out of hits. But it took two Indian pitchers to blank him. However, the wonder and memory of that fabulous streak will warm the hearts of baseball fans for all time. And with good reason. During those fifty-six consecutive major league games DiMaggio pounded out 91 hits in 223 times at bat, batted in 55 runs and scored 56 times.

SUPERMAN
IN A HURRY

WHEN JESSE OWENS was an unknown boy in high school, he had no inclination for sports. His name might have been buried in obscurity for the rest of his life if it had not been for a kindly school teacher who advised the frail-looking, shy Negro boy to go out for the track team because he thought it would do him good. Reluctantly, and with no enthusiasm for the sport, skinny Jesse did. From that curious beginning, Jesse Owens went on to carve his name and fame into sports history as one of the greatest track and field athletes of all time. He became an Olympic immortal. By winning four gold medals in the 1936 Olympic Games, he turned in one of the greatest Olympic performances of all time.

However, when Jesse Owens was a twenty-one year old sophomore at Ohio State University, he achieved a feat never equaled by any other track and field athlete in history.

On the afternoon of May 25, 1935, Jesse Owens came to Ann Arbor, Michigan, to compete in a Big Ten Conference track meet, featuring the outstanding college athletes of the nation.

He had come to that track meet feeling unwell. He had a sore back, and he was reluctant to compete in more than one event.

Nevertheless, at precisely 3:15 o'clock, Jesse flashed down the track to win the 100-yard dash, and tie the world record of 9.4 seconds.

At 3:25 he took his first and only broad jump of that day. He cleared 26 feet 8¼ inches, to set a new world record.

At 3:45 Jesse sped down the track to win the 220-yard dash, in 20.3 seconds. He broke the accepted world record for the event.

At 4 o'clock Owens climaxed his unbelievable one-man performance by sprinting over the 220-yard low hurdles in 22.6 seconds, to shatter another world record.

Thus, within the space of less than one hour, the incredible Jesse Owens broke three world records, and tied another. The fortunate ten-thousand spectators who crowded the wooden stands on that historic day to see that superman perform his fantastic show could hardly believe what they saw.

THE HUMAN FROG

THE MOST PROLIFIC winning Olympian of all time is perhaps the least remembered. Ray C. Ewry won so many championships in the Olympic Games that his record run of victories became monotonous.

In his boyhood, he was an invalid; his family despaired of his life, but the doctor suggested that Ray might build up his frail body through exercises. Weakling Ray Ewry turned to track, and he began to specialize in jumping. In time, he not only improved his health, but he also developed a pair of long, steel-springed legs which made him famous as a "Human Frog." No one could beat him in a contest of the standing high jump, the standing broad jump and the standing hop, step and jump.

In 1900, when he was twenty-seven years old, he first appeared in Olympic competition. At the Olympic Games in Paris, Ewry won the standing high jump, the standing broad jump and the standing hop, step and jump. He returned home with three gold medals.

However, that feat marked only the beginning of his incredible record run of Olympic victories. In 1904, when the Olympic Games were held at the World's Fair in St. Louis, the tall lanky American again performed as a "Human Frog" for Olympic glory. Again he won the same three events. Once more, he emerged with three gold medals.

Two years later, when the Olympic Games were held in Athens, Ray Ewry was again competing against the world's foremost jumpers. He won the standing high jump and the standing broad jump championships. Now, he had an unprecedented eight gold medals.

But the amazing "Human Frog" was not yet done with Olympic triumphs. In 1908, at the Olympic Games in London, there was Ray Ewry, again jumping against the world's best. He was then more than thirty-five years old. Nevertheless, he won the standing high jump, and the standing broad jump championships, to capture two more gold medals.

He never again competed in the Olympic Games. But his fame was secure forever. He had won ten Olympic championships in all and ten gold medals—three more than any other athlete has ever won in the history of the Olympic Games.

FROM HERO TO GOAT

BIG ED AT BAT

ON OCTOBER TENTH, the last day of the 1904 big league baseball season, John Dwight Chesbro, the star pitcher of the old New York Highlanders now the Yankees, made a wild pitch, with two out in the ninth inning of a game with the Boston Red Sox, and it cost the New York club the game — and the pennant!

This was the stunning climax to the greatest season ever achieved by a modern major league hurler.

With each passing year, Chesbro's accomplishment in the 1904 pennant campaign appears less likely to be equaled. In that season, he went to the mound fifty-three times, and he won an incredible total of forty-one games.

This was his heroic record as he let go the wild pitch on the final play, on the final day of his most glorious season.

In sports, costly mistakes are recalled long after remarkable achievements are forgotten. Nevertheless, John Chesbro's forty-one victories in a single season will never be matched.

EDWARD J. DELAHANTY is now in baseball's Hall of Fame. The most famous of five brothers who all played in the big leagues, he was one of the greatest first basemen in history, and the equal of most any slugger. In the sixteen years he starred, he compiled a .346 lifetime batting average.

During his career, the handsome and merry Irishman, nicknamed "Big Ed," performed many unforgettable feats. But he accomplished one batting record that set him apart in baseball history.

In 1899, when he played with the Philadelphia Phillies, he hit .408 to win the batting championship of the National League. In 1902, when he starred for the Washington Senators, he hit .376 to win the batting title of the American League.

Thus, he alone captured the batting championships of both major leagues.

A strange tragedy ended Big Ed Delahanty's career. During the 1903 season, while still at the height of his power he mysteriously drowned at Niagara Falls.

The record he left behind as a batting champion of both major leagues is not likely to occur in present-day baseball.

GAME WITHOUT END

SINCE BIG LEAGUE BASEBALL began, in the nineteenth century, thousands upon thousands of major league games have been played. The longest major league diamond contest was fought on May 1, 1920.

There was a faint drizzle in the air on that Saturday afternoon when Umpire Barry McCormick called, "Play Ball!" to start the game between the former Boston Braves, now of Milwaukee and the former Brooklyn Dodgers, now of Los Angeles. A slim gathering of only 2,000 fans huddled in the stands of the Braves' ballpark to see the regular scheduled game. Joe Oeschger was on the mound for the Braves, and Leon Cadore was pitching for the Dodgers. Neither pitcher was a top hurler of his time; neither of the two had an inkling that destiny had brought them together on that dreary afternoon to create the greatest iron-man pitching feat of all time.

"Let's get this game over in a hurry!" yelled little Rabbit Maranville, the Braves Hall of Fame shortstop to his teammates, as the lead-off Dodger hitter stepped into the batter's box. But that game was to go far beyond the usual nine innings of play; it was to last ten minutes shy of four hours before it came to a finish, with no winner and no loser.

Nothing important happened until the first half of the fifth inning when the Dodgers scored a run. The Braves scrambled to even the count, doing so in the last half of the sixth inning to tie the score at 1-to-1.

Thereafter, the two rival pitchers settled down to scoreless hurling, and the zeroes began to extend across the scoreboard. At the conclusion of nine full innings of play, that game was still deadlocked at one run for each team.

As that game went into extra innings, the two rival pitchers disdained relief; for each was grimly

| Dodgers . . . | 000 | 010 | 000 | 0 |
| Braves . . . | 000 | 001 | 000 | 0 |

determined to win. And so that May first contest dragged on and on, and after nine more full innings of play, the score still remained deadlocked at 1-to-1.

The two rival pitchers completed the nineteenth and twentieth innings, still going strong. The enthralled crowd watched that fantastic marathon stretch itself into the longest major league game ever played. Rally after rally was snuffed out without a run.

The tension was tremendous as the two teams completed the twenty-first, twenty-second, twenty-third and twenty-fourth innings. And still the score remained deadlocked at one run each. The two starting pitchers, Joe Oeschger and Leon Cadore, breezed through the twenty-fifth and twenty-sixth innings — achieving the greatest feat of "iron man pitching" ever seen in a baseball game. While Cadore had hurled twenty successive innings for his team, Oeschger had pitched twenty-one shutout frames for his club — a record for consecutive scoreless pitching in a single game that still stands! It was the longest pitchers' battle, by innings, in major league history. Curiously, each team had used only eleven players throughout that grueling contest.

It took an umpire to terminate the unprecedented baseball game. At the finish of the twenty-sixth inning when the ball was hardly visible against the gray clouds of the cold, damp day, umpire McCormick called the game because of darkness, with the score still tied at 1-to-1.

Disappointed, the weary players straggled out of the ballpark. There was no winner and no loser in that baseball game of May 1, 1920, but the players of the two teams had performed an impressive feat. In a single afternoon, they had played a record-making twenty-six innings — the longest baseball game in big league history!

				R	H	E
00	000	000	000	00 --1	9	2
00	000	000	000	00 --1	15	2

BANTAM BEN'S COMEBACK

AT THE BEGINNING of the year of 1949, Ben Hogan was a symbol in the sports world. His name meant wizardry and perfection in every phase of the golf game. Son of a humble blacksmith in Texas, bantam Ben was the world's greatest golf player. The former caddie boy had been the first to achieve the American Golf Slam, by winning the National Open, the P.G.A. title, and the Western Open in a single year. He had captured every major golf championship in the United States, and he was the top money winner of his time.

However, on February 2, 1949, disaster came, and it was all over for golf champion Ben Hogan. Driving home on a fog-shrouded lonely highway, he crashed head-on into another automobile. When little Ben was dragged out of the twisted metal to be rushed to a hospital one hundred miles away, he was more dead than alive. His collarbone, ankle and several ribs were broken. His pelvis had been fractured, his legs and hips had been badly hammered, and he had suffered internal ruptures. His survival was a medical miracle.

No sooner had he weathered the crisis, than thrombosis developed in his smashed leg, nearly necessitating amputation. An emergency operation saved his left leg. Then, a blood clot developed in his right lung. More emergency surgery saved his life.

Pessimists feared that courageous Ben, who had to lie flat on his back for months, might never walk normally again. No one believed that ever again would he play golf. But with fanatical determination, the tight-lipped Texan did both. Amazingly, he returned to the golf wars to match strokes with the greatest players in the world. Fans by the thousands stampeded the fairways to marvel at the incredible little man who was trying to reclaim his throne as the king of all golfers.

In June of 1950, although his scarred legs were still bandaged from knee to ankle and walking was difficult for him, Ben Hogan startled the golf world by entering play for the United States Open Championship. His staunchest admirers believed that his heart was much bigger than his battered and weary body. All keenly felt the impending embarrassment Hogan would suffer now playing in golfdom's most grueling test.

"He'll be lucky if he ever again breaks 80," said most of the players who once fearfully had fought against him. But they did not know the real Ben Hogan, with the indomitable will to win. He outplayed the world's top pro and amateur golfers, and he captured that Open title by four strokes. It was an unbelievable feat.

But bantam Ben's incredible comeback was not yet complete. As time went by, twice more he won the U.S. Open championship, and in 1953, he performed another unparalleled feat. He became the first player ever to score the triple sweep of golfdom — winning the U.S. Open, the Masters, and the British Open, in a single year.

Little Ben Hogan came all the way back from the brink of death to the loftiest golfing heights. His rare courage won universal admiration.

TWO STUBBORN MEN

THE MOST unusual nine-inning no-hitter took place on May 2, 1917 at Wrigley Field, between the Chicago Cubs and the Cincinnati Reds. Two rival hurlers pitched that no-hitter, and strangely, both pitched it in the same nine innings of play. It not only was baseball's greatest pitching duel, but it also became the only major league game in history in which two teams completed nine full innings without one hit.

On that historic afternoon, huge Fred Toney was on the mound for the Cincinnati Reds. Jim "Hippo" Vaughn was pitching for the Chicago Cubs. Those two bitter mound rivals were the two burliest hurlers in the majors; together, they packed more than five hundred pounds of beefy weight.

As the game progressed, the slim crowd of 3,500 spectators in the stands sensed that the two behemoths were about to engage in a fantastic pitching duel. But no one imagined how unbelievable it was going to be. Inning after inning was to be recorded on the scoreboard with neither pitcher giving up a single hit.

After nine full frames of play, both men had hurled a no-hitter; a twin pitching achievement beyond belief. A miracle had come to pass.

In the tenth inning, Fred Toney lumbered out to the mound and pitched another hitless frame. But in the last half of that tenth inning, Jim Vaughn finally faltered. A lucky hit and a lucky error lost the game for him, by a score of 1 to 0.

Thus baseball's greatest pitching duel came to an end. But as long as big league baseball is played, that game will be remembered. In that amazing diamond contest, Fred Toney and Jim Vaughn hurled the only twin nine-inning no-hitter in major league annals.

IT BEGAN AND FINISHED IN MAY

ON THE AFTERNOON of May 6, 1915 a twenty-year-old rookie pitcher named George Herman Ruth, playing for the Boston Red Sox, hit his first major league home run. It caused not a ripple of interest or comment. That season, the young pitcher wound up with only four homers but eighteen pitching mound victories. The following season his home run slugging still evoked no gasps of admiration, for while winning twenty-three games, he had belted only three more homers. The 1917 season was similar; again he won twenty-three games as a pitcher but hit only two homers.

However, in the 1918 season, when the promising young pitcher, Babe Ruth, hit eleven home runs, the baseball world began to notice him as a slugger. He was even pursuaded to give up pitching and become an outfielder, so that he could play every day and perhaps hit more home runs.

Thus began the most incredible home run saga in baseball history! The former pitcher began to generate the greatest slugging power ever seen in the majors. As the seasons went by, he hit home runs in such abundance that it stunned, awed and delighted his fans.

In each of seven seasons Babe Ruth hit more than forty homers. In each of three seasons, he hit more than fifty homers. And in the 1927 season, while playing in only 151 major league games, he set an astounding all-time record of sixty home runs. Seventy-two times, Babe Ruth hit two homers in a single game, to set another all-time record that may stand forever! Babe Ruth's home runs earned him everlasting fame as the "King of Swat" and made him the most famous baseball player of all time!

It was a curious twist of fate that brought the immortal player to his final glorious moment of home run hitting on another day in May.

On May 25, 1935, forty and weary, Babe Ruth gave the baseball world something to remember him by. The most colorful and colossal slugger of all time was playing out his major league streak with the mediocre, habitually tail-end, former Boston Braves. The game was against the Pittsburgh Pirates. Babe Ruth came up in the first inning to a mighty ovation. He quickly acknowledged the crowd's acclaim as he swung at the first pitch, connected, and sent a tremendous long home run over the right field fence.

When the body-sore and leg-weary old Babe came to bat for the second time, again he connected, and slugged the ball over the right field wall for another long home run.

In the fifth inning Ruth came to bat for the third time, but he only hit a single. However, when he came to bat in the seventh inning for his fourth time in that game, the crowd hushed into a curious and respectful silence. What more could old, washed-up Babe Ruth do that day to recapture some of the glory of his youth?

The answer came in a violent outburst. After taking two quick strikes, Babe Ruth again connected and hit his third home run of the game. It was one of the longest home runs ever seen!

The thousands of fans in the stands rose up as one and gave Babe Ruth one of the greatest ovations ever accorded a ballplayer. But no one in that crowd realized the sadness of that moment It was the last home run Babe Ruth was ever to hit. A few days later, he retired from the game.

From his first home run in the major leagues, which he hit on a day in May, to the last home run he hit on another day in May, twenty years later, Babe Ruth had created the most fantastic home run hitting saga in baseball history! Babe Ruth had slugged an incredible total of 729 home runs in major league competition.

TOP OF THE WORLD

IT WAS THE lifelong ambition of Edmund Hillary to climb up to the highest point a man could go and still keep his feet on ground. He hoped to become the first man to conquer the peak of the world, Mount Everest.

When that determined Australian was thirty-four years old, he finally reached his goal. In frightful cold, on May 28, 1953, he inched up to the summit of ice-crusted Mt. Everest and stood among the clouds on the roof of the world's highest mountain, 29,028 feet above sea level.

Edmund Hillary's heroic conquest of Mount Everest, towering more than five miles high, not only was an epic triumph in man's eternal battle against nature, but it also was an astounding feat in the ancient sport of mountain climbing.

FIVE DERBIES
FOR EDDIE

WHEN THE five feet and three inches, 114-pound George Edward Arcaro was riding race horses to fame and fortune, he was beyond any question the greatest American jockey of modern times. A native of Cincinnati, Ohio, he was only thirteen years old when he became an exercise boy and stable hand at a race track. He was hardly fifteen when he became a full-fledged jockey. His beginning was ludicrous. He fell off horses, and often he was left at the post. He rode more than one hundred races before he managed to pilot home his first winner.

Arcaro's early years as a professional jockey were a blend of blood, pain, hunger, ridicule, tears and heartbreak. Many were the times when he narrowly escaped sudden death beneath thundering hoofs. He suffered broken bones, caved-in ribs, and long visits to hospitals. However, with the passing years, "Heady Eddie" rose in reputation and riches, until he became the world's most colorful and greatest jockey. He also became a millionaire.

He rode horses until he was forty-six and became a turf legend. He won 549 stake races. He won the Triple Crown of turfdom seventeen times. He wound up with 4,779 winners, and a money-earning record of $30,039,543.

Of all the feats that gained for Eddie Arcaro everlasting fame his riding in the Kentucky Derby was his greatest triumph. The traditional annual "Run for the Roses" has been America's most famous, glamorous, and important horse race since 1875.

It was on May 7, 1938, when Arcaro was given his first big break at Kentucky Derby fame. He was offered "Lawrin" to ride. No one believed the mount had a chance to win. But "Heady Eddie" piloted the long-shot to a sensational victory to capture his first Derby crown.

In the 1941 "Run for the Roses" Arcaro had a leg up on "Whirlaway" — a colorful thoroughbred feared as a man-killer and ridiculed as one of the dumbest horses in racing history. Courageously and skillfully, he rode the horse to a first place finish by eight lengths and a new track record — to pick up his second Derby winner.

For the 1945 Derby race, Arcaro was astride "Hoop Jr." Through mud and slime, he galloped home to victory, to win his third Kentucky Derby. Only two other jockeys in history ever achieved a triple triumph in America's most famous horse race.

But Eddie Arcaro was not yet done with Derby winning. In the 1948 race, he piloted "Citation" to a roaring victory, to pick up an unprecedented fourth Derby winner.

Then in 1952, once again "Heady Eddie" galloped home a winner — this time "Hill Gail" — for his fifth Kentucky Derby triumph. It completed the greatest feat of turf riding in history. His record of incomparable jockey horsemanship may stand unmatched forever.

SEVEN FOR SEVEN

ONLY ONE PLAYER in history ever made more than six hits in a single nine-inning major league game. Wilbert Robinson, a one-time catcher, achieved that greatest of all hitting feats on a June day in 1892. It was a baseball record that probably will stand unmatched forever.

On the afternoon of June 10 in the season of 1892, Wilbert Robinson, one of the great backstops of his time, went behind the plate to catch for the old Baltimore Orioles in a game against the National League St. Louis club. As usual, catcher Robinson batted in the eighth slot for his team, just above the pitcher. It was to be just another routine game between two big league teams going nowhere on the pennant trail. But Robinson's phenomenal hitting turned that ballgame into a memorable contest. No one in the history of baseball has ever had a more productive day at bat than Wilbert Robinson.

From the first inning the game seemed something of a fiasco. The Baltimore Orioles went on a rampage, piling up twenty-five runs to St. Louis's four in the nine innings played. But the most outstanding Oriole player of the day was catcher Wilbert Robinson, who came to bat seven times. Each time, he hit safely, rapping out six singles and one double. His "Seven for Seven" in that nine-inning game set a venerable all-time record and made catcher Wilbert Robinson unique in baseball history.

END OF THE RAINBOW FOR PAPPY

SINCE MEN BEGAN to fight with padded fists for fame and fortune, prizefighting has been a rugged sport limited to the young. But one old ringman, Jersey Joe Walcott, scored a victory that went down in boxing history.

Joe Walcott, born Arnold Cream, became a fighter when he was only sixteen years old to escape from the misery and poverty of a dreary boyhood. Although he started out as a promising pugilist, he found neither fame nor fortune in the ring. It was a grim struggle for him to gain recognition as a prizefighter. For years he was ignored, neglected, discredited and cheated by all.

To eke out a meager livelihood at his brutal trade he was forced to travel all over the world and fight in obscure places for small purses. Six times he quit the ring in bitter resignation at his inability to build a ring career for himself. At the age of thirty-one Jersey Joe Walcott found himself a weary, disillusioned, penniless prizefighter, and he quit the ring to dig ditches, collect garbage and work as a stevedore or bricklayer. At times, he also had to seek public relief to house and feed his wife and six children. A deeply religious man, he accepted his poverty and hardships as the will of God.

But happily for Walcott, he was induced to return to the ring for one more comeback. This time, somehow, after many years of frustration, his ring career began to prosper. Jersey Joe managed to punch out with his fists a reputation sufficient to land him four different title bouts for the world's heavyweight championship. Each time, he failed to win this most prized crown. However, sincere faith in himself kept Walcott going as a fighter.

"God wants me to be a champion," said Walcott, "why else would I be given so many chances at the title?"

On July 18, 1951, when Jersey Joe Walcott was thirty-seven and a half years old, he was given his fifth and final opportunity to fight for the world's heavyweight championship. The cynics laughed: Walcott s chances against young defending champion Ezzard Charles seemed absurdly slim. He was too old, too tired and too far out-classed by the champion who twice had already beaten Walcott easily. When the bell sent the two men into action, old Jersey Joe Walcott was grimly determined to put up the fight of his life.

In the early rounds he tried to take command by digging sharp left hooks into the champion's body, followed with jolting rights to his head. But the young champion came back with explosive blows savagely pounding Walcott's weary body. Thus it went for six hard-fought rounds.

Early in the seventh round as the two combatants were sparring at long range, a miracle happened that was to change the course of boxing history. Walcott fired a tremendous left hook that caught the champion flush on his jaw. Ezzard Charles fell forward, collapsed on the ring floor and was counted out.

While thousands of frenzied spectators rose to their feet roaring a thunderous acclaim of the "pappy guy" who was champ, humble Jersey Joe Walcott fell on his knees in his corner, and, weeping unashamedly, prayed in gratitude for the miracle his fists had wrought.

Jersey Joe Walcott had become the oldest fighter in history to win the heavyweight championship.

HOTTEST MAN ON ICE

WHEN GORDIE HOWE was a little boy living in the tiny Canadian prairie town of Floral, Saskatchewan, he received his first pair of ice skates through an act of charity. His family was on relief, and shortly before Christmas, a kind woman came to his impoverished home bearing gifts for the poor. In her sack, filled with old clothes and second-hand toys, young Gordie happily found a pair of rusty old skates and a hockey stick.

He was a gangling teenager of only fifteen when he reported to the tryout camp of a big league hockey club. He was told to go home and advised to give up his foolish notions that he would ever make pro hockey's Big Time.

However, when Gordie was barely eighteen, he was signed up by the Detroit Red Wings of the National Hockey League. He was one of the youngest players to crash big league professional hockey.

As the years went by, Gordie Howe became not only a super star of the National Hockey League, but also he came closest to being the "complete" hockey player. A master in all departments of the game, he became almost a one-man hockey team. He gained an unmatched reputation for strength, toughness, and durability. The capers he cut on ice rinks, competing against the world's greatest hockey players, were beyond compare.

Over the years, the indefatigable star of the Detroit Red Wings collected more honors than any player in professional hockey. He became the first performer to reach a total of 1,000 points in regular-season play. He scored more goals than any other player in history.

In 1962, when the veteran Gordie Howe was thirty-five years old, and in his seventeenth Big Time season, he captured the National Hockey League scoring championship for the sixth time. No other player had led the league in scoring more than twice. Even more amazing, he won the National Hockey League's "most-valuable-player award" for a record sixth time.

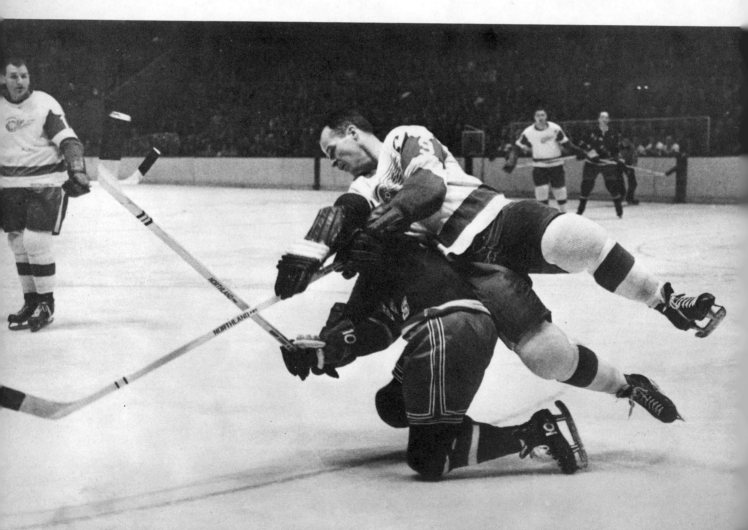

THE LONGEST
FIST FIGHT

EVER SINCE PRIZE FIGHTING began as a sport centuries ago, countless men the world over have fought in the ring for fame and fortune. But the greatest endurance feat of the sport was achieved by two lightweights, Andy Bowen and Jack Burke. They met in the ring on April 6, 1893, at the famed old Olympic Club in New Orleans. Those two 133-pounders had agreed to fight to a finish for a purse of twenty-five-hundred dollars, plus a side-bet of one-thousand dollars. The winner was to receive a shot at the world's lightweight championship.

It was the most grueling fist fight with boxing gloves ever fought in the prize ring. On it went— ten, twenty, thirty, forty, fifty rounds but neither little man gave nor asked for quarter. Fiercely, grimly and stubbornly they battled through each three-minute round.

The fight dragged on far into the night. It reached sixty rounds, then seventy; on to eighty, passed ninety, and up to one hundred rounds, and still the game fighters fought on.

Finally, after fighting continuously for seven hours and nineteen minutes, for a total of 110 full three-minute rounds, Jack Burke and Andy Bowen had grown so weary, and were both so badly battered that each refused to come out of his corner, for the 111th round. So, the referee made a difficult decision. He called off all bets, and declared that marathon bout to be "no contest."

GRANDMOTHER WAS A BOWLER

FOR CONTINUED EXCELLENCE in a sport, no other female athlete in history has matched the record of Marion Ladewig.

In 1950 she won the world's bowling championship for the first time, and thirteen years later she still dominated the distaff side of the tenpin game as the reigning Queen of the bowling world.

In 1963, when she was past forty-eight years, the bowling grandmother won the two most important individual tourneys, the All-Star and the World Invitational, to retain her title as the world's female bowling champion. Moreover, she captured the honor of "Bowler of the Year"—for the tenth time. Her unprecedented record is an impressive one.

IT WAS SUNDAY AFTERNOON of November 8th, in the 1970 National Football League season, when the powerful Detroit Lions tangled with the weak New Orleans Saints. The Lions were overwhelming favorites to win that game by a lopsided score, and high were their hopes to capture the league championship by that season's end.

However, to the surprise of the 69,810 spectators watching that contest, the mighty Lions barely held the lead by a score of 17-to-16 — with only eleven seconds of play left in the game, and with the Saints in possession of the ball on their own 37-yard line. There was time for only one more quick play.

Then onto the playing field came the Saints' 23-year-old star punter Tom Dempsey. Already, he had kicked three field goals, and now his team was calling upon him to kick another field goal from an incredible distance for a victory. It seemed to be an impossible mission.

But unruffled, quickly and calmly, Tom Dempsey swung his right foot against the ball and sent it flying into the air, straight and clear through the goal posts, for a winning field goal.

It was the greatest field goal ever kicked by a big league pro football player — the longest winning field goal ever seen in football history. Tom Dempsey's field goal measured exactly 63 yards!

Perhaps even more unbelievable was Tom Dempsey's role as the heroic punter for the longest field goal in the history of professional football. For he had been born deformed, with a stub where one of his hands ought to be, and with a part of his right foot missing. To gain his fame as a kicking specialist in the violent world of pro football, he used an artificial right foot encased in a specially designed football shoe. Yet, despite his great handicap, during the 1970 football season he accomplished the most memorable and most glorious kicking feat ever achieved by a big league pro football player.

THE PHANTOM FINN

NO MODERN NAME in track history breathes a more storied eminence than that of Paavo Nurmi of Finland. He was the greatest distance runner of all time and the most prolific record maker the sports world has ever known. No other man ran so many foot races over so many different distances, and remained unbeatable for so many years as did Nurmi.

In his heyday he demolished at least nineteen world records from 1,500 meters to 20,000 meters. Also, while running in many strange lands against the world's foremost runners, he racked up innumerable national, international, and Olympic records.

Born in 1897, Nurmi had an unhappy boyhood. Before he was twelve, he was orphaned and had to leave school to go to work. His boyhood idols were Finland's most famous runners, and he dreamed of a time when he, too, would be hailed as a champion foot racer. He dedicated himself to that dream, and to train himself as a runner, he embarked on a Spartan conditioning program. In time, he learned to run with flowing ease and grace, like a mechanical man.

In 1920, when Nurmi was twenty-three, he competed for the first time in the Olympic Games at Antwerp, Belgium. He was beaten in his first race, the 5,000 meter run. But undiscouraged, he came back to win the 10,000 meter race, and lead Finland's team to a victory in the 10,000 meter cross-country event.

Four years later, in the 1924 Olympic Games in Paris, France, the "Phantom Finn" astounded the world. On one afternoon, within only ninety minutes, the incredible Nurmi competed in the 1,500 meter race and the 5,000 meter event. Never before had an Olympic athlete even dared to attempt such a grueling running feat. But he not only won both races, he also set an Olympic record for each event.

However, he was not yet done as the all-conquering hero of the 1924 Olympics. He won the 10,000 meter cross-country race, and he led Finland's relay team to a record-shattering victory in the 3,000 meter race. Only he emerged with four gold medals.

Four years later, in the 1928 Olympic Games in Amsterdam, the aging Flying Finn won his final Olympic foot race, by capturing the 10,000 meter championship. Paavo Nurmi had won a total of seven gold medals. No other runner in history has won so many Olympic championships.

He came to the United States in 1925 for a national tour of the indoor board tracks, against America's foremost and swiftest runners. On January 8 of that year Nurmi ran his first race in America. It also was the first race he ever ran indoors. Nevertheless, he not only won with ease, but he set a new world indoor record.

The next night, he ran another race, a thousand miles away. Again he won, and again he set a new world record. Thereafter, almost every time he ran during his strenuous tour which spanned the whole country, Nurmi hung up a new record. In his first twenty-four days in America, he set sixteen new world records.

During his invasion of America, superman Nurmi ran sixty-nine races. Although always pitted against the nation's top runners he won sixty-eight times. Even more unbelievable, he glamorized that awesome string of wins by setting thirty-eight new records.

No runner ever matched the record making exploits of the immortal Paavo Nurmi, the greatest distance runner the world has ever known.

FELIX THE FOURTH

FELIX CARVAJAL was a postman in Havana, Cuba, when in 1904, he learned that the Olympic Games of that year were to be held as an adjunct to the World's Fair in St. Louis, Missouri. Stirred by patriotism, the impulsive little Cuban became convinced that he was a great runner, destined by fate to win the Olympic marathon race for the glory of his country. Inspired by his crazy dream, he paid no heed to the sober truth that he had never run a competitive foot race, to say nothing of the fact that he had never run the marathon distance of 26 miles and 385 yards.

Since Cuba had no intention to send any of its athletes to participate in the 1904 Olympics, and since he had no money to finance an expedition of his own to the United States, he embarked on a simple plan to change that. Daily, he would run around the great public square in Havana to attract attention to his running skill. When a crowd gathered, he begged for contributions to help him finance a trip to the Olympic Games. By such repeated performances he collected enough money to overcome his financial plight.

Late that summer, he sailed to America to compete in the Olympic marathon. But alas, he went by way of New Orleans. During a brief stopover in that gay city, Felix was waylaid by gamblers and enticed into a friendly dice game. He was suckered out of all his money.

Although stranded in a strange city, broke and friendless, Felix was still determined to compete in the Olympic marathon. So he set out on foot to run all the way from New Orleans to St. Louis — a distance of 700 miles.

He ran with little rest or sleep, eating whatever food he could beg from farm houses along the way. It was a grim, lonesome foot race against time and distance. Finally, he reached the site of the Olympic Games, only a few hours before the start of the marathon race.

Worn, weary, and half-starved, Felix came up to the starting mark for the marathon, the queerest-looking specimen of an Olympic runner ever seen. He was wearing heavy walking shoes, a long-sleeved shirt, and long trousers. The crowd roared with laughter.

A friendly athlete with a pair of scissors snipped off the sleeves of Felix's dirty shirt, and cut his trousers in half to give him some semblance of a track man.

On August 30, under a broiling sun, and in stifling heat, the marathon race started with thirty of the world's greatest long-distance runners. The thirty-first runner was Felix Carvajal who had no experience in competitive running, knew nothing about pace, and never had raced in a marathon.

By the half-way point, the scorching heat of the day, the choking dust of the roads, and the brutal strain on leg, heart, lung and muscle took a heavy toll. Runner after runner dropped exhausted to the ground, unable to continue. But the tiny Cuban tirelessly jogged along the course. Only fourteen finished the race. Felix Carvajal was one of them. He was in fourth place.

In Olympic history, Felix Carvajal is not glorified as a marathon champion. But, in the sports world, he will always be remembered as "Felix the Fourth," the most magnificent loser in the history of the Olympic Games. To place fourth in a twenty-six mile run he ran over 700 miles.

THE MIRACLE
THAT FAILED

THE GREATEST STRETCH of "perfect" pitching baseball has ever seen was in May, 1959.

On the night of May twenty-sixth, in Milwaukee's County Stadium, pitcher Harvey Haddix warmed up for the Pittsburgh Pirates. Haddix wasn't feeling very well: for several days he had been nursing a nagging cold and he wished he were back at the hotel in bed. But although he was running a slight temperature and his nose was so clogged that he found it difficult to breathe, he was ready to give out with everything he had. Game little Harvey Haddix had always been that kind of ballplayer.

The southpaw probably had only one thought in mind during those early innings against the Milwaukee Braves — to get the game over with as quickly as possible. He thought he would be lucky to last through the fifth inning. But when the fifth rolled around, the Braves had yet to get their first hit from the veteran Pirate hurler. A light rain had started to fall and an occasional

flash of lightning rent the sky. Some of the fans even left the ballpark to escape the threatening elements; their misfortune was to miss one of baseball's most dramatic shows.

As inning after inning was recorded on the scoreboard it became evident that a pitching miracle was in the making. Haddix had not allowed the slugging Braves to get a single man to first base. At the end of nine full innings of play he had mowed down twenty-seven batters in a row to complete a "perfect no-hit, no-run game." In all of baseball history, only seven major league pitchers before him had hurled perfect nine-inning no-hitters.

But Haddix hadn't yet won that game. His teammates had failed to score a single run for him, and his perfect no-hitter went into extra innings. However, the magic of his arm kept the miracle going for the awed crowd in the stands. Alternately blowing his nose and blowing fast balls past the Braves batters, he didn't allow a single hit or walk in the tenth inning, nor in the eleventh and not even in the twelfth!

The fans knew they had already seen baseball history. No one had ever before pitched a "perfect game" for more than nine innings. No one had ever pitched a no-hit game for more than eleven innings. Harvey Haddix had exceeded both records. Yet, he still had to win his game.

In the last half of the thirteenth inning, disaster struck: an error ruined that "perfect game," and a long hit ended it. The final score was 2-0. It was a heart-breaking climax to a pitching masterpiece.

SEVEN PASSES TO GLORY

IT HAS BEEN SAID that no other position demands as many skills as that of the quarterback on a football team. Football history has recorded the astonishing feats of many superlative quarterbacks, but the title of forward pass wizard belongs to Sid Luckman.

In his time, he was something of a gridiron phenomenon. Unlike many other football greats, Sid Luckman rose from the sidewalks of New York to gain fame as a college football hero and later as a professional grid star. His forward passing, during the twelve years he played for the Chicago Bears of the National Football League, not only rewrote the record book, but also changed the appearance of the game of football itself. With quarterback Luckman at the helm, the famed Chicago Bears made the T-formation their dominant offense system.

As one of the finest quarterbacks of all time, Sid Luckman had many "field days" to his credit. But on the afternoon of November 14, 1943, he produced a "first" for football history!

On that memorable Sunday, the undefeated Chicago Bears were challenged by the powerful New York Giants; it was a contest between the world's greatest football players. A record crowd of more than 57,000 spectators thronged New York's historic Polo Grounds. Most had come to pay tribute to Sid Luckman, the home town boy who had become an immortal big league quarterback. A grateful Sid Luckman turned that "welcome home" occasion into a monumental performance of forward passing, which, to this day, serves as a goal for every great quarterback.

Midway in the first period of the game, he rifled a spectacular forward pass to a teammate who proceeded over the goal line for a touchdown. On the final play of the first quater, Luckman struck again with a pin-point fifty-four yard aerial pass, and before the first half had ended, the ace quarterback had scored his third and fourth touchdown forward passes of the game.

That New York's most famous football son was humiliating New York's own great football team and inflicting upon the Giants the worst defeat in their history meant little to the roaring crowd. The hometown fans yelled for more of Luckman's forward passes.

Early in the third period, he hurled a towering fifty-five yard pass on the fly for his fifth touchdown pass. When he was benched for a rest, the frenzied spectators roared: "We want Luckman! Send in Luckman!"

So back into action went Sid Luckman to continue his fantastic aerial circus. He threw his sixth forward pass touchdown of the game, and before it ended, he hurled another to set a new all-time record for forward passing in a single game.

The famous ballpark known as the Polo Grounds where, on November 14, 1943, quarterback Sid Luckman achieved the greatest feat of forward passing in football history no longer stands. But as long as football is played, Luckman will be remembered as the first player ever to throw seven touchdown forward passes in a single game, an incredible exploit of precision forward passing that may never be equalled.

THE NORWEGIAN DOLL

In the spangled world of figure ice skating, the most dazzling performer was a Norwegian girl immortalized in sports history as Sonja Henie.

She was only six when she first began to learn the art of navigating on ice skates, in her hometown of Oslo. She was so clumsy and had so many spills that her parents were advised to take her skates away before she broke her neck. But in 1924, when the chunky and spunky Sonja was eleven years old, she won Norway's women's figure skating championship.

In 1927, when the tiny, blond, doll-like Norwegian girl was hardly fifteen years old, she captured the women's figure skating championship of the world. She held the title for ten consecutive years. It was the longest championship reign in the history of the sport.

In 1928, while still fifteen, Sonja won her first Olympic Games figure skating championship. Four years later, she was again crowned the Olympic queen of figure skaters, and four years after that, she once more won the championship title in the Olympic Games. No female athlete in history ever lasted as long as a champion in Olympic competition as the incomparable five-foot "Norwegian Doll."

Capturing the Olympic figure skating crown three consecutive times and winning the world's figure skating championship for ten years in a row, Sonja Henie won unchallenged fame.

When Sonja Henie was twenty-three, she finally relinquished her fabulous reign as the world's figure skating champion, and for the following twenty years, she performed all over the world as a professional ice skater. No other figure skater ever attained her universal popularity, and she earned more money than any other male or female athletic performer in history. Her figure skating artistry earned a fortune of over fifty million dollars.

BOY WONDER OF BILLIARDS

BILLIARDS was created in the fourteenth century for the diversion of kings and princes and ladies and gentlemen of the royal court. In time, it became a popular game for the world's masses. Down through the years, untold millions of people have played billiards, one of the most scientific of games. Unquestionably, the greatest player of all time was America's Willie Hoppe.

He was only five years old when he started to play on a battered billiard table that stood in the back of his father's barber shop in Cornwall on the Hudson. By the age of eleven, he was so skilled with a cue stick that he was touring the country playing exhibitions against the top billiard players in the land. The "Boy Wonder" was the nickname Willie Hoppe received for his youthful fame.

When he was barely eighteen, he challenged France's Maurice Vignaux, then the billiard champion of the world, to a duel for the title.

For years the fabulous "Old Lion" had reigned undefeated.

On January 15, 1906 the two met in a 500-point match for the world's billiard championship, in the glittering Grand Ballroom of the famed Grand Hotel in Paris. An overflow crowd of distinguished spectators gathered from all over the world watched the contest. Fortunes were wagered on the outcome of that match.

In one of the most staggering of upsets, Willie Hoppe won and became the billiard champion of the world. To prove that his accomplishment had been no fluke, the "Boy Wonder" began to roam all over the globe matching his skill against the world's greatest cue masters, at any style of billiard play. He won hundreds of titles, and as he grew older, he became known throughout the universe as "Mr. Billiards."

In 1952, Willie Hoppe captured his last world billiard title. It completed the most durable championship reign in all sports history. From his first to his last title, he had been a world's billiard champion for forty-six years in a row.

For a sports champion, it is a longevity record without equal.

THE SAGA OF SEWANEE

DURING THE 1899 football season, the Sewanee football team from the University of the South embarked on a back-breaking journey to win gridiron glory. An undefeated football team, Sewanee undertook to play five games in five different cities many miles apart—against five of the most powerful college football teams then in the game. Sewanee agreed to play all five games within a period of only six days!

In the first game, Sewanee played an unbeaten Texas University football team, and won by a score of 12-to-0. The next day, after traveling many miles by horse and wagon, Sewanee played the powerful Texas A. & M. team and won again —this time by a score of 32-to-0.

After another long trip, Sewanee played its third consecutive football game in three days against the mighty Tulane University team, and again, Sewanee won—by a score of 23-to-0.

The following day was Sunday, a time for prayer and rest. However, the day after, Sewanee resumed its grueling grind, this time licking an undefeated Louisiana State University team, 34-to-0.

And the very next day, again after a long drive, Sewanee challenged a powerful Mississippi State team, and won again, this time by a score of 12-to-0.

That completed Sewanee's record-breaking journey—playing five football games in five different cities, against five powerful football teams —in only six days! Astonishingly, Sewanee not only won all five games, but also shut out all of its opponents without a score. It was truly an incredible feat of gridiron ruggedness!

But what made that feat even more memorable was that the Sewanee football squad had only eleven players in all — no substitutes. Those rugged Sewanee players came from a tiny college with a student body of only ninety-seven men.

THE HUMAN POGO STICK

WHEN SIBERIAN-BORN Valeri Brumel was a boy of fourteen in the obscurity of the smoky city of Voroshilovgrad, he began competing in track as a high jumper. By the time he was eighteen, the young Russian was being acclaimed all over the world as the greatest high jumper in history.

In 1961, young Brumel set new world indoor and outdoor records for the high jump event. His most phenomenal leap of that year measured seven feet four inches.

While on a visit to the United States in the summer of 1962, Russia's incredible jumping-jack stunned the largest crowd in track history with a fantastic high jump leap: clearing the high bar at a height of seven feet five inches, he eclipsed his own world record.

The world believed that the ultimate had been reached in the high jump. But Valeri Brumel was not yet done with his magic way of soaring into the air. On September 29, 1962 in Moscow's Lenin Stadium, he was to perform his greatest leap.

Strangely, he came to that exciting event with a hole in his shoe. Just prior to the track meet, fabulous Brumel discovered a hole in one of his shabby spiked track shoes. When he rushed to a nearby shoemaker to have it repaired, he was told that it couldn't be done. He wangled a piece of twine from the shoemaker and managed to mend the shoe himself.

On that historic afternoon, wearing his patched shoes, Valeri Brumel tried twice to surpass his own world high jump record, but failed each time.

Nevertheless, when he stepped out on the field for his final jump of the day, the crowd of 70,000 spectators rose as one to give the idol of the Russian masses a standing ovation. The handsome, world-famous youngster slowly raised his hand above his head, but it was not a hero's salute to the frenzied worshippers who were exhorting him to perform the impossible. It was merely a signal to the officials near the pit that he was about to start his last leap.

His first few steps toward the high bar seemed like a lazy walk to nowhere. But suddenly, Brumel was moving fast. His six-foot, 175-pound body hurtled into the air, and then he was clear and falling into the pit, face up, leaving the cross-bar untouched above him. He covered his eyes for fear that the bar might yet fall and destroy his greatest feat, but the hysterical roar of the crowd told him that he had accomplished the high jump of all time. His fantastic leap had carried him over the crossbar at a height of 2.27 meters—seven feet, 5¾ inches!

As space historians will long remember the world's first Russian cosmonaut, so will sport historians commemorate Valeri Brumel who at the age of twenty had already jumped higher than any other man.

THREE'S A CROWD
—ALWAYS

IT HAPPENED in a World Series. The date was October 10, 1920, when an undistinguished second baseman in one play became a baseball immortal. He had the tongue-twisting name of William Wambsganss.

It was the fifth game of the 1920 series. The Cleveland Indians and the Brooklyn Dodgers were tied at two games each. In the top half of the fifth inning, Pete Kilduff was the lead-off batter for the Dodgers. He hit a single. The next batter, Otto Miller, did the same. With baserunners on first and second, now up to bat came pitcher Clarence Mitchell, a feared hitter.

At that moment, Cleveland's second baseman Wambsganss, motivated by a curious whim, moved out to play his position more than ten feet deeper into the field than usual. Mitchell slammed the first pitch for a screaming line drive.

It was traveling more than fifteen feet to the right of second base, and almost nine feet above the ground. It looked like a sure two-bagger.

Out of nowhere came Wambsganss shooting into the air for a glove-hand catch. The catch was spectacular in itself, but nothing to what followed. When he came down to earth, Wambsganss saw Kilduff had strayed far from second base. So, he stepped on the bag, doubling him up for the second out. Then he spotted Miller near second, scrambling back toward first. Immediately, he gave pursuit, and the chase ended when Wambsganss put the ball on Miller for the third out of that historic inning.

Second baseman William Wambsganss had written an otherwise undistinguished name in the record books — the only man in World Series history to make an unassisted triple play.

THE WONDER RUNNER IN HIS GREATEST RACE

IT WAS ON September 6, 1960, in Italy's Eternal City, Rome, that Australia's "wonder runner" Herb Elliot toed the mark for the Olympic Games 1,500 meter run. Though the lean twenty-two year old kid held the world's record for the mile, at 3:54.5, and had recorded 3:36 for the 1,500 distance, he was no odds-on favorite to win the glamor race of the Olympics, for he had been out of competition for two years. No one in that huge crowd in Rome's Olympic Stadium thought that Australia's hawk-faced wonder miler would win easily.

True, he was the only man in history to run the mile seventeen times under the magic four minutes. Still eight of the world's fastest milers were running against him for the 1,500 Olympic championship. Most of them already had accomplished a sub four-minute mile. Herb Elliot had hung up his spikes two years ago, and said it was for good. He had been so weary of running for fame, that he had even turned down a startling quarter-million dollar offer to run professionally. Now, after two quiet years away from the limelight, he was coming back to run one more race.

When the 1,500 meter race started, the great miler made no effort to take the lead. At 200 meters, he was running in third place. At 300 meters, he was tied for fifth place, running easily on the outside; at 800 meters, he was still in fifth position. It didn't look as if he would eclipse the Olympic distance record of 3:41.2. It didn't even look as if he could win.

Then, without warning and catching all the other runners by surprise, Herb Elliot made his move. He spurted into the lead, his stride smooth and powerful. The field stretched out behind him. At the one-thousand meter mark, he was timed in 2 minutes, 25.4 seconds. And still, he continued to pile it on, showing no signs of tiring.

The roar of the crowd of 100,000 spectators was deafening, as Herb Elliot opened up an eight yard lead. The killing pace was too much for his competitors, great as they were. They were running against a man who was in a frightening hurry to make history—and he did. Elliot finished more than twenty yards ahead of his nearest competitor. Not only had he won, but he had shattered his own world record for distance.

It was the most exciting 1,500 meter race in history, the first six runners to cross the finish line smashed the Olympic record. And Herb Elliot, the winner, was clocked in the unbelievable time of 3 minutes, 35.6 seconds. This would be the equivalent of a 3:52.6 mile.

This was the race that capped a fabulous track career. Elliot achieved a feat that may never be topped by another runner.

A DIVE TO FAME

Of all the female divers in sports history, Pat McCormick from Long Beach, California, was the greatest. Once, in only six seconds, she dived into immortality as an aquatic champion for the ages.

In 1952, pretty Pat emerged from the Olympic Games as a double gold medal winner. She won both diving championships, to be acclaimed the world's greatest performer in springboard competition, as well as the greatest woman diver America ever had.

But Pat McCormick wanted still more. In 1956, when she was a twenty-six year old housewife and mother, she traveled to Melbourne, Australia, to compete again in the Olympic Games. Effortlessly, she won a third gold medal in the springboard event. But Pat yearned to become the first mermaid to capture four Olympic championships. Fate seemed to be against her. When she climbed the thirty-foot platform in the outdoor Olympic aquatic arena for the final diving event, she had only two optional dives left in which to achieve her victory. She was trailing the field in fourth place, and it was unbelievable that her final two dives would top those of the world's greatest distaff divers who were competing against her.

The Olympic pool, jammed with thousands of spectators from all over the world, froze into a hushed silence as Pat poised herself on the small diving platform, three stories above the water. Suddenly, she took off into space, and executed a difficult two-and-a-half dive that was so breathtaking, beautiful and flawless that even the judges of the contest applauded her performance.

For her final optional dive, Pat executed a startling one-and-a-half with a full twist. It took defending champion Pat McCormick only six seconds to execute the two greatest dives ever performed by a woman. They earned for her all the points she needed to win her fourth gold medal.

Those six seconds of splendor made Pat McCormick unique in Olympic history. Her double-double diving championship feat in two sets of Olympic Games immortalized her as the only woman in sports history who ever captured four individual Olympic championships.

HERO WITHOUT SHOES

THE MARATHON run originated with the Greek runner Pheidippides who in 490 B.C. ran from Marathon to Athens to announce a victory over the Persians. He climaxed his heroic act by gasping, "Rejoice, we conquer!" and falling dead. When the Olympic Games were revived in 1896, that historic occasion was commemorated with a marathon race over the original route of 26 miles and 385 yards which once had been run by Pheidippides. Ever since then, hardy long distance runners have been running marathons for fame. But the man who ran the greatest and most unbelievable marathon was Abebe Bikila of Ethiopia.

He was a skinny twenty-eight year old unknown soldier in the Palace Guard of Emperor Haile Selassie. Although he had never before run a marathon race, in 1960, he came to Rome, Italy, to compete in the Olympic Games. Pitted against the world's greatest marathon runners, Abebe Bikila was not only considered a rank outsider but also a ludicrous contender.

Nevertheless, he not only amazed the world by winning the Olympic marathon, but even more incredible, he ran the fastest marathon race known. He was clocked in 2 hours, 15 minutes, 15.2 seconds.

However, the most unbelievable part of that fantastic competition was that Abebe Bikila ran the entire grueling distance of 26 miles and 385 yards barefooted. Four years later, the amazing barefooted wonder Abebe Bikila again won the marathon race at the Olympic Games, to become the first and only man in history to win two Olympic marathons in a row.

SLAUGHTER
ON THE GRIDIRON

SINCE FOOTBALL BEGAN in America in 1869, thousands of teams have competed for glory on the gridiron. But a team from Georgia Tech rolled over its opponents to rack up the highest football score ever recorded.

On October 7, 1916 on Grant Field in Atlanta, Georgia Tech played Cumberland College. One thousand curious spectators were on hand to observe the skirmish. The famed "Rambling Wrecks" from Georgia Tech were then coached by John Heisman, one of football's hallowed names.

That afternoon, Georgia Tech was an angry football team bent on working off a grudge against its opponent, for the preceding spring, an athletic team from Cumberland had humiliated Tech in a baseball game.

Cumberland punted to start the game, and on the first play from scrimmage, Georgia Tech scored a touchdown. It was to be the first of many. When the score reached 28-to-0, the over-powered Cumberland team changed its strategy. Instead of receiving the ball after each Georgia Tech score, it elected to kick off, thus keeping the "Rambling Wrecks" in their own territory. But it did no good. The score continued to mount and the first quarter ended with Georgia Tech ahead by a score of 63-to-0.

The bewildered Cumberland team took refuge in holding the ball as long as possible, determined to keep the score down. Nevertheless, the first half ended with the score 126-to-0.

In the second half, the rampaging Georgia Tech players scored almost every time someone got the ball. Midway through the third quarter, Tech's right end ran for yet another touchdown, and the score mounted to 154-to-0. It set a world's scoring record for a single football game. And still the slaughter went on.

Finally, after forty-five minutes of play, with the battered and bruised Cumberland players near total exhaustion, the two rival coaches agreed to stop the game. By that time, Georgia Tech had amassed 528 yards rushing and returned punts for 220 yards and kickoffs for 220 yards. The final score of that brief football game was 222-to-0.

MILE-A-MINUTE MURPHY

IT IS BELIEVED that the sport of bicycling actually started with a Frenchman named M. de Sivrac when in 1690 he first appeared on the streets of Paris, riding a crude, two-wheeled contrivance. In time, millions upon millions of people throughout the world took up bicycle riding for necessity, recreation, and sports fame.

Down through the years, bicycle racing has produced many remarkable champions whose names will glow forever in the history of this sport. However, the cyclist who accomplished the most unforgettable feat was an American named Charles C. Murphy.

Shortly before the beginning of the twentieth century, when bicycle racing was flowering into its Golden Age, Charles Murphy was a cyclist noted for his ruggedness, durability and speed. But he became the laughing stock of the sports world because he believed that someday he would pedal a bicycle at a mile a minute.

To attempt the impossible, Charles Murphy persuaded the Long Island Railroad to build a three-mile wooden track between its rails, over a level stretch of ground near the town of Hempstead. A train was to pace him over a measured mile, in a bicycle race against time.

On June 30, 1899, Murphy mounted his bicycle and took off behind a train. By the time the marked mile was reached, the train was going sixty miles an hour. And cyclist Murphy was right behind it. Pedaling furiously, he raced across the measured mile in the astonishing time of 57-4/5 seconds. It was an unbelievable, new world's bicycle speed record.

His whizzing ride caused a universal sensation. Almost overnight, he became famous throughout the world as "Mile-a-Minute" Murphy. As the fastest bicycle rider in history, he reaped a fortune in exhibitions.

As a bicycle champion, "Mile-a-Minute" Murphy left behind him no enduring speed records. But because of his single remarkable feat, his name towers above those of the most famous cycling champions. He was the first athlete in history to prove that a human being could pedal a bicycle at a speed of better than a mile a minute.

HER COURAGE CREATED A LEGEND

DURING HER LIFETIME, Mildred "Babe Didrickson" was an amazing one-woman track team; twice she was crowned a track champion at the Olympic Games. She was an unbeaten sprinter, hurdler, broad-jumper and high-jumper, as well as an expert javelin and discus thrower. Babe was an outstanding performer in more than a dozen different sports. This versatility earned her universal acclaim as the greatest all-round woman athlete of all time.

But the greatest sports feat Mildred ever achieved was in golf. It is a classic story of grit, stamina and guts.

The incomparable Babe turned to golf, winning her first tournament in 1940, and from there, she went on to capture the next twenty major golf tournaments in a row, to set an all-time victory record. The first American to win the British Women's Amateur championship, Babe won ninety big-time golf titles in all before she turned professional. She was to earn more money than any other woman golfer in history.

Yet one triumph stands out above all the others in Babe's spectacular career. On July 3, 1954 when Babe came to the long, difficult, wind-blown course of the Salem, Massachusetts Country Club to compete in the U. S. Women's Open, she was only a shadow of her former self. The greatest woman athlete in history was weary and sick. At forty years of age, she had not long to live. Little more than a year before, surgeons had labored desperately to arrest the ravages of the dreaded cancer that was destroying her.

No one believed that Babe Didrickson would ever play golf again. But that amazing lady had iron-willed herself out of the hospital and with indomitable courage had returned to the golf circuit.

As that U. S. Women's Open began, not even the most optimistic person believed that the physically unfit Babe would be able to withstand the grueling rigors of a difficult championship course. Seventy-two holes were to be played in only three days, with a back-breaking thirty-six hole game on the final day.

Fighting an erratic wind and occasional rain, uncomfortable because of the tube and kit she carried next to her ravaged body, equipment made necessary by corrective surgery, Babe turned in two of the most polished rounds of her fabulous career—72 the first day, and a subpar 71 on the second day. She led her closest rival by six strokes going into the final thirty-six hole ordeal.

On that last day of play Babe achieved an unparalleled golfing feat; her triumph should represent a beacon of courage and hope for all the handicapped.

Despite a hazardous wind, Babe went out that morning and completed the eighteen hole round in 73 strokes. But the final eighteen holes were to be sheer torture for her. Each step became more and more of an effort. She completed the first nine holes in an incredible 36 strokes, but the back nine she played by instinct alone. Her struggle against exhaustion was evident in every swing. Fatigue flooded Babe's body, but she refused to give in to it, finishing the game with a score of 39 strokes for a final round score of 75.

Her last shot made, the Babe had to be helped off the final green. Her total score in winning the 1954 U. S. Women's Open was 291, a shotmaking miracle. She had won that exhausting tournament by twelve strokes, the largest margin ever achieved by a player in major golf competition!

Yet this victory involved more than an accumulation of strokes by a player of unmatched skill. It was the most heroic feat in the annals of golf, scored by a woman deep in the shadow of death. Babe Didrickson never played golf again, and only two years later she died, leaving behind a priceless legacy of talent and courage that is now the brightest legend among the greatest golf feats of all time.

THE BEAST OF PRAGUE

EMIL ZATOPEK began as a self-taught runner. When he was an unknown soldier in the Army of tiny Czechoslovakia, he spent all of his free time running up and down the rugged hills of his country. He always ran the hard way—wearing his heavy hobnailed boots and his soldier's pack. His Army comrades thought he was crazy, especially when he told them that he was training to become the world's greatest long distance runner.

When the frail-looking Zatopek first appeared in an official track meet, people laughed at him. His clumsy running form was the worst ever seen on the cinders. When he ran he rolled his head, waved his arms, gnashed his teeth, and gulped for breath. Startled track experts stared at him with disbelief and said that he ran like a man who had been stabbed in the heart. Graceless Emil Zatopek was nicknamed the "Beast of Prague."

Nevertheless, in the 1948 Olympic Games, he surprised all by plodding in his grotesque style to a victory in the 10,000 meter race and setting a new Olympic record for the event. He became the first Czech ever to win an Olympic championship. It was a miracle for a freak runner.

Four years later, at the 1952 Olympic Games, in Helsinki, Finland, the "Beast of Prague" stunned the sports world with an unbelievable feat.

In the grueling 10,000 meter race, Zatopek not only outran thirty of the world's swiftest distance runners but he floundered over the six-mile course in the astonishing time of 29 minutes and 17 seconds. It was a new Olympic record!

Next, the tireless Czech with the wretched and grotesque running form ran to a victory in the 5,000 meter race, in only 14 minutes 6.6 seconds, shattering another Olympic mark.

However, two gold medals and two Olympic records still were not enough for the glory-hungry "Beast of Prague." On the last day of the Olympic Games, he decided to run in the marathon race. It hardly mattered to him that he never before had run the marathon distance of 26 miles and 385 yards, nor did it worry him that he was not given the slightest chance to win. Zatopek ran fifty-two of the world's finest marathoners into the ground and won the race by the margin of more than half a mile. In winning the first marathon race of his life, he was clocked in the remarkable time of 2 hours, 23 minutes and 3.2 seconds. Never before had a man run a faster Olympic marathon.

Thus, Emil Zatopek, the most ridiculed runner in Olympic history, within seven days, not only won the three most taxing long distance foot races in the 1952 Olympic Games, but he also set a new Olympic record for each event.

THE QUICK HAT TRICK

THE RECORD SET by Bill Mosienko, right-winger for the Chicago Black Hawks back in 1952 may never be challenged. The veteran hockey player scored three goals in an incredibly short span of time.

The game itself between the New York Rangers and the Black Hawks was of little significance. It was the final one of the regular season, and the few fans who drifted into Madison Square Garden on that March night were probably just seeking a dry place to escape the wind and the rain. They could hardly have anticipated much excitement.

They were right. For two periods, the skaters put on a routine performance. Then, without warning, Mosienko took a pass and cut straight in at the Ranger goal. He faked goalie Lorne Anderson to the left and flipped the puck along the ice onto the right side of the nets. Time: 6:09. A few seconds later, Mosienko had the puck again and was weaving through the Ranger defenses. He shot and scored. Time: 6:20.

At the ensuing face-off, Chicago took possession of the puck. It was relayed to Mosienko who headed goalward once again, hesitating long enough to bring the Ranger goalie scrambling out of his cage. Then Mosienko let fly, and the puck went true! Bill Mosienko had scored 3 goals in only 21 seconds! After a moment of stunned silence, the crowd leaped to its feet and cheered one of the greatest achievements in the annals of big league hockey, a record that will be long-remembered and may never be broken!

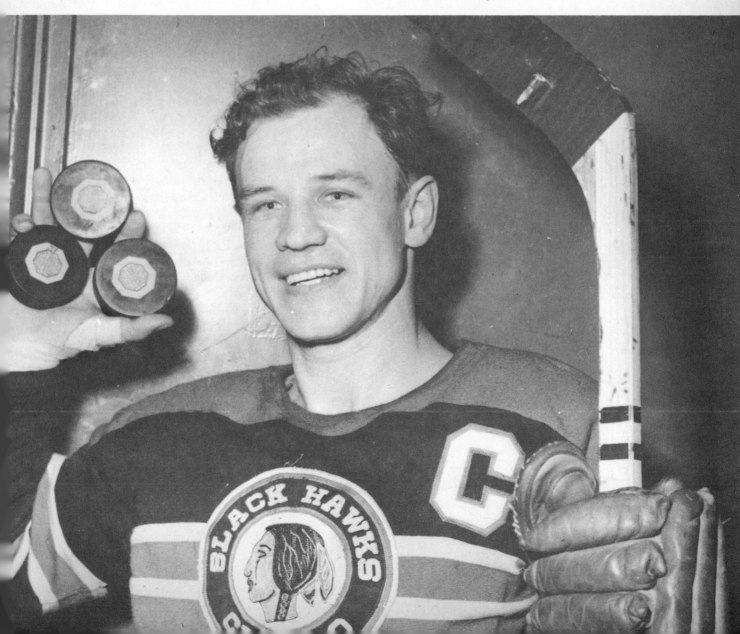

FIVE BOOTS TO PAY DIRT

IN HIS TIME Bob Waterfield was one of the greatest quarterbacks and forward pass artists in football history. But oddly enough, in a game against some of the greatest football players in the world, he created gridiron history, not with his unerring right arm but with his powerful right leg.

It happened on a sun-kissed December afternoon in 1951, in the vast Los Angeles Memorial Coliseum, before a crowd of 70,000 frenzied spectators. The Los Angeles Rams played the powerful Detroit Lions in a "must game" for both teams. It was a contest to decide the Western Division league championship. The Rams were depending on their brilliant quarterback Bob Waterfield to mastermind and forward pass them to a victory. Instead, he gave them his foot.

The game was only a few minutes old when the Rams' attack faltered within sight of the goal line. Bob Waterfield booted the ball through the uprights from the seventeen-yard line for his first field goal of the day.

Midway in the second quarter of that exhausting contest, the Rams' attack stalled again. Calmly, quarterback Waterfield kicked the ball through the goal posts, this time from forty yards away, for a second field goal. Time was running out in the first half when he booted another three pointer, from the twenty-five-yard line, his third of the day.

In the second half, Bob once more kicked the ball to pay dirt, from the twenty-yard line. His fourth field goal tied a National Football League record for a game, shared by the most illustrious kickers in pro football history.

But Bob Waterfield was not yet done with his phenomenal footwork. Before the game ended, he booted one more, this time thirty-nine yards away from the posts, for his fifth field goal of the game.

It completed the most incredible kicking exhibition in big league pro football history and made Bob Waterfield unique in the annals of the game. He became the first and only player in National Football League history to kick five field goals in a single game.

A LONELY SEA VOYAGE

On october 20, 1956, Hannes Lindemann of Germany, set out on a strange sea voyage. His goal was to cross the Atlantic Ocean in his tiny boat, only seventeen feet long and piloted by a crew of only one—himself.

He sailed from the Canary Island harbor town of Las Palomas, and ended his voyage in the harbor town of Phillipsburg in St. Martin—seventy-two days later. During the entire trip, he was alone at sea. He rarely slept for longer than an hour at a time, as he fought against the winds, the storms, thirst, hunger, and all the dangers of the sea. But he was rewarded for his effort. He achieved an historic "first" in man's ancient battle against the sea. Never before had the vast Atlantic Ocean been crossed in so small a boat, piloted by one man alone.

WILT THE STILT

IN THE BEGINNING, Wilt Chamberlain was something of a problem. As a boy, he was a bother to his poor family and a joke to his neighborhood. By the time he was twelve, he had grown so tall that his father had to raise the ceiling light fixtures in their home so that Wilt wouldn't bump his head against them. He needed a special, long bed to sleep on, and too quickly he grew out of the large-sized special clothes bought for him. Boys of his age refused to play with him; he was too big for their games. When Wilt was only fifteen, he towered six feet ten inches tall.

When he tied on a pair of sneakers for the first time to play schoolboy basketball, he was regarded by all who played against him as a big goon. But he soon proved himself to be a most efficient basketball player. By the time he was ready for college, he had become the object of the wildest competition in the history of collegiate athletics. He received free scholarship offers from 150 colleges! The 7-foot 1-inch Wilt Chamberlain soon became the most publicized college basketball player of all time.

When he turned professional to play with the Philadelphia Warriors of the National Basketball Association, at the highest salary ever paid a basketball player—$65,000 a season—many basketball purists still regarded him as merely a sideshow oddity and cynically scoffed at his potential as a court performer. They believed that the sensational Wilt "The Stilt" would quickly be cut down to size playing in big league competition. Although the twenty-one year old Wilt was only a rookie, he wasted no time in casting his awesome spell over the greatest basketball players in the world. In his first big league season, he took more shots, scored more points, made more goals, got more rebounds, took more free throws, and played more minutes per game than any other player in basketball history.

In his first campaign as a pro player, Wilt Chamberlain broke the single season scoring record of 2,000 points with ease. The season after, he became the first player in history to score more than 3,000 points.

Basketball players and coaches who became unwilling victims of Wilt Chamberlain's devastating point-making orgies, prophesied that some day this giant would accomplish the most "impossible" scoring feat in big league basketball.

That day came Friday, March 2, 1962, when in Hershey, Pennsylvania the Philadelphia Warriors played a scheduled NBA game against the New York Knickerbockers. A sparse crowd of 4,124 spectators turned out to see that historic game in which Wilt Chamberlain gave the most unbelievable display of scoring ever witnessed. From the outset, the giant began to score with deadly shots from all angles, and before that game was many minutes old, it became evident that Chamberlain was determined to make shambles of all previous one-game scoring records in basketball history. As Chamberlain's famed fallaway shot repeatedly found its mark, the Knicks concentrated their defense around him, and two, three or even four men ganged up on him. To escape the ignominy of Wilt's onslaught, the New York five fought desperately. They stalled, fouled and pulled every trick in the book to prevent him from receiving passes from his teammates, but almost every time Wilt got his hands on the ball, he scored.

At the end of three periods of play, he had scored sixty-nine points. As the final period began, he quickly passed his own all-time scoring mark of seventy-three points for a regulation game.

The tension reached a peak as the excitement of Chamberlain's scoring orgy swept the crowd in the stands. Loudly and wildly, the fans began to chant: "Give the ball to Wilt! Give it to Wilt!"

With seven minutes of play remaining in the game, Wilt eclipsed his own all-time record of seventy-eight points which he had set in an overtime contest on December 8, 1961. And still he continued to score.

With five minutes left to play, he reached point number eighty-nine. With only one minute and nineteen seconds left to play, he grabbed a high pass and dunked in his ninety-eighth point. Then, Wilt took two more quick shots at the basket, but missed both. Forty-six seconds were left to play. The amazing giant grabbed a pass, jumped high, and with both hands stuffed the ball into the basket for his hundredth point of that game!

Wilt Chamberlain had achieved the "impossible," and in so doing had smashed nine records as he scored thirty-six field goals and twenty-eight free throws.

No basketball player ever had a greater day. The prophecy which had followed Wilt Chamberlain ever since he first began to play basketball was fulfilled. He had hit one hundred.

97 PITCHES

MANAGER CASEY STENGEL had told him that he was going to pitch the fifth game of the 1956 World Series. However, twenty-seven year old Don Larsen, a mediocre hurler for the fabulous New York Yankees all season, was neither jubilant nor worried over his assignment to face again the feared Brooklyn Dodgers. He had started the second game but lasted less than two innings. Stengel's decision was certainly open to question.

Three years before, carefree Don Larsen had come to the major leagues with great expectations and quickly floundered while gaining a dubious reputation as a playboy. One season he had posted one of the worst pitching records in history, losing twenty-one games for the Baltimore Orioles. But Lady Luck was to be kind to him. In a mammoth seventeen-player deal, the biggest swap in baseball history, Larsen was traded to the Yankees. However, with the greatest pennant-winning club of all time, erratic Don remained a losing pitcher.

On the afternoon of October 8, 1956, he casually sauntered to the mound to pitch the key game for the world baseball championship. He wasn't worried about his past failures and indiscretions. He simply wanted to pitch a winning game that might save his job.

Without even the benefit of a windup, tall Don pitched effortlessly, breezing through the early innings. His fastball was steaming, and his control was perfect. By the end of the seventh inning, no Dodger batter had made a hit or reached a base. The awed 65,000 spectators in the vast Yankee Stadium began to ask if a baseball miracle were in the making. But it was preposterous to hope for a no-hitter in a World Series. It couldn't happen, certainly not in a championship contest against a team that boasted some of the mightiest sluggers then in baseball.

Unperturbed, Don Larsen pitched through the eighth inning unscathed.

At the start of the ninth inning, the Yankees led 2-to-0. Twenty-four Dodgers had been retired. Larsen needed only three more outs to complete the greatest pitching performance in World Series history.

Carl Furillo, a batting champion and the Dodgers' great clutch hitter was the first to face Larsen in the ninth. He fouled off four pitches before lifting an easy fly to the outfield. Next to bat came mighty Roy Campanella, the greatest home-run hitting catcher in the history of the Dodger club. After he had belted a long drive into the stands that went foul by inches, Larsen forced him to hit a weak infield grounder for an easy putout.

With two down, Dale Mitchell, a dangerous pinch-hitter, came to bat. Larsen's first pitch to him was a ball. The next was a strike. Then a fastball roared into home plate for strike two. But the next pitch was fouled into the stands, and the screaming crowd froze into a frightened silence. Cooly, Larsen got set. The next pitch was his ninety-seventh of that game, and it was to be his last. A fastball flashed by the surprised batter, cut the outside corner of home plate, and thudded into the catcher's mitt. The game was over.

On that historic day Don Larsen had hurled the first no-hit, no-run game in World Series history. In his perfect no-hitter, he had faced twenty-seven men and had retired them all in order—with no hits, no runs, no walks.

For Don Larsen that perfect no-hit, no-run game was the greatest and most glorious victory of his life, an exploit unlikely to be equaled.

THE GRAND SLAMMER

DON BUDGE did not take to tennis naturally. As a freckle-faced redheaded youngster growing up in California, he liked all the other sports better. Hitting a tennis ball bored him. Until nearly fifteen, he hardly touched a tennis racket. Only because he had been egged on by an older brother, Don entered his first tennis tournament. To his surprise he won it. The tennis bug bit him when he captured his first trophy, and Don was hooked for tennis glory.

As time went by, gaunt long-limbed Budge mastered every shot in the game—the complete tennis player. Before Don was twenty, he was acclaimed one of the greatest players in the world. He had rarely lost a match.

In 1938, when Don was twenty-two, he reached the highest pinnacle ever attained by a tennis player.

Budge began the 1938 tennis season by winning the Australian national championship, even though at the time, he was plagued with the discomfort of a temporary loss of voice.

From the Land of Down-Under, he hopped across the world to France to play for the French championship. Although he was suffering an intestinal disorder, he swept the French title.

Then Don went to England to play for the famed Wimbledon championship. Against the world's greatest players, he took the British title without the loss of a single set.

With three of the most coveted world's amateur championships in his possession, the amazing redhead took a "breather" from individual glory, to help his country defend the fabled Davis Cup, the symbol of the world tennis championship. Don led the United States Davis Cup team to a smashing victory over Australia.

His "duty" gloriously fulfilled, he came to historic Forest Hills to play for the American national championship. Again, he faced the world's foremost players. For the first time in his life, he began to suffer with insomnia. But once on the court, Don Budge settled down to his "perfect" form and walked away with the title.

By sweeping the four major world's amateur championships in a single year, Don Budge became the first man in tennis history to score the "Grand Slam" of tennisdom.

To appreciate the scope of his feat, consider that it took twenty-four years before another great tennis champion matched Don's four-pronged triumph. But Grand-Slammer Budge is still the only American male to win, in a single year, the world's four top tennis championships.

A BUNCH OF CINDERELLAS

IN THE LONG HISTORY of major league baseball, many once hopelessly beaten teams have made heroic and spectacular comebacks against insurmountable odds—to win pennants. But beyond any doubt, the greatest pennant-win of all was achieved by the New York Giants in 1951. They performed the most fantastic Cinderella act in the history of the national pastime.

As late as August 11 in that pennant campaign, the faltering Giants were completely and thoroughly out of the race for the National League flag. At the end of that day, the front-running Brooklyn Dodgers were leading the league by an overwhelming margin of 13-½ games.

But the Giants' dapper, brawling, talkative manager, Leo 'Lippy' Durocher, refused to accept the inevitable. He made his bedraggled Giants believe that they were a bunch of Cinderellas in wait for the golden chariot to take them to the world series ball.

On August 12, the foolish Giants began to believe in fairy tales, and as the days passed, they ripped off sixteen victories in a row.

However, by September 21, the amazing Giants had whittled down the Dodgers' lead to four-and-a-half games in the winning column and six in the all-important losing column. They now had only seven more games to play to finish the season. They won all seven, while the proud but demoralized Dodgers unexpectedly began to stagger down the homestretch as the baseball-world looked on in disbelief. The Dodgers lost twice to the Philadelphia Phillies, fell twice before the Braves, and still another loss erased the 13-½ game lead which had been theirs on August 12. The Giants and the Dodgers finished that 1951 season deadlocked for the pennant.

So, the two teams played a best of three game playoff series for the flag. The Giants won the first game and the Dodgers the second. In the third and final contest, coming into the ninth inning, the Dodgers led by a score of 4-to-1. The Dodgers were now only a few steps away from the end of the rainbow.

As if by magic, the Giants' Al Dark singled. Mueller, the next batter, also singled. A teammate popped out, but Whitey Lockman sliced a double to left to score a run. It brought up to bat Bobby Thomson, with two men on base, and two runs behind. The tall Scot became the Prince Charming for the Cinderella Giants. He hit a home run into the stands! That homer heard round the world was perhaps the most dramatic home run ever hit. It completed the miracle of Coogan's Bluff—winning for the 1951 Giants a pennant that couldn't be won! A bunch of diamond Cinderellas had achieved the greatest pennant-winning feat of all time. It could never happen again—unless you believe in fairy tales.

THE GREAT DOUBLE "300"

It was the night of June 22, 1959. Ed Lubanski, bowling star and former minor league baseball pitcher, peered down the alley at Miami's Bowling Palace and set himself for a try at an historic goal, two consecutive 300 point games, two perfect games in a row! It had never been done in bowling history!

Already that evening, Lubanski had aimed his ball twenty-three times. On each try, all ten pins went down. One more strike and he would have bowled his second consecutive perfect game!

One 300-point game is considered spectacular enough in championship competition. Two was unheard of. After Lubanski's first 300 score, the gallery figured he'd cool off, lose that fine edge. But they reckoned not with his immense pride and discipline. Lubanski was playing a hot hand. He had picked up the gauntlet and come back for more. Eleven more strikes followed, each greeted with a roar that comes only when spectators are acutely aware that history is unfolding before them.

Lubanski needed one strike to accomplish what had never before been achieved. Two consecutive perfect games. Twenty-four consecutive strikes.

As he readied himself for his final effort, Lubanski was painfully aware of the tension permeating every corner of the vast hall. The pressure of the moment was compounded by the force of the hundreds of pairs of eyes focused on him, waiting to see if he could take the final step in his total destruction of previous bowling records. He gripped his ball, resting it in his left hand, as he studied the pins. Then he made his move.

He approached the foul line, the ball swung back, almost shoulder high. It arched forward. The sound of its roll filled the Bowling Palace. Straight to its target between the number one and number three pins it rolled. Then all ten pins went spinning down. In that split second, Ed Lubanski had taken a giant step beyond every bowler in history.

A wave of noise swept around him. An event had taken place which no one ever expected to see, two consecutive perfect games. Twenty-four consecutive strikes. It was the greatest bowling feat in the annals of that sport.

A ROCKET WITH A RACQUET

RODNEY GEORGE LAVER began swinging a tennis racquet when he was ten years old. His father, a cattle rancher in Rockhampton, Australia, was his first tennis teacher. At thirteen, he was already playing in tennis tournaments against men. But at fifteen, he was sidelined from tennis-playing because of a serious case of jaundice. When he recovered, he left home to work more than four hundred miles away, for fifteen dollars a week, plus an opportunity to play lots of tennis.

A famous Australian tennis coach took him under his wing, and helped develop him into an international amateur tennis player. At eighteen, that 68-inch left-handed redhead was the world's best junior tennis player, and at twenty-four, he was the world's greatest amateur male player. He became the second player in history to achieve the "Grand Slam" of tennis. Curiously, Rod Laver who was universally famed as "the Rocket" didn't even look like a great tennis champion should. Pixieish, with a freckled boyish face and a pigeon-toed walk, he looked like a misplaced ballboy on a tennis court. But when he began playing, he was one of the most explosive tennis performers ever seen. The speed, power and skill of his shots were awesome. The greatest tennis players in the world were no match for him.

In 1963, with no more amateur tennis worlds to conquer the flaming Rocket became a touring tennis professional for his fame and fortune. Surprisingly, in the beginning he was a flop as a money-player. He lost 21 out of his first 23 pro tennis matches. But it didn't break his spirit. Before long, he found the magic and gold in his racquet, and he became acknowledged monarch of the tennis world. Year after year, always playing against the world's greatest racquet swingers, his prize-winning earnings were astronomical.

In 1971, when he was thirty-three years old, little Rod Laver was not only still on top of his game as the world's top tennis player, but he also achieved the greatest money-winning feat of all time. In that single year, he won more money than any tennis player in history — $292,717. And he raised his career winnings to over one million dollars — thus becoming the first tennis player in history to achieve such a millionaire distinction, in proof of his imperishable greatness as the ultimate pro tennis champion of all time.

OPENING DAY FOR A FELLER

DOWN THROUGH THE YEARS, many big league baseball seasons have been launched with spine-tingling, heart-pounding, and unforgettable Opening Day performances. Bob Feller made inaugural day headlines on April 16, 1940.

Chicago, the Windy City, was living up to its reputation. There were only 14,000 shivering fans in Comiskey Park on that cold, gusty afternoon to watch the home town White Sox begin their season against the Cleveland Indians. Right-hander Bob Feller was the principal reason for even that many spectators appearing for that Opening Day contest. The twenty-one year old Feller was no longer a schoolboy wonder. He had grown up and was now ready to inscribe his name among the pitching immortals.

Bobby hadn't been too keen for the honor of pitching that initial game. Before it began, he had complained of a stiffness in his arm, and he didn't feel very well. He hoped that he would last nine innings.

Because it was difficult to make a curve break with a strong wind at his back, Bobby relied entirely on his famed fast ball. Although the opposition was stubborn and his control wavered at times, he hurled his way through inning after inning, never in serious trouble. Between the fourth and eighth innings, he downed fifteen consecutive White Sox hitters. He came into the ninth inning atop a 1-to-0 score. Even more amazing, he had not given up a single hit to the opposition.

In the last half of the ninth, Bobby faced the heart and power of the White Sox lineup. He had no difficulty disposing of the first two batters. Then up to bat came hard-hitting Taft Wright, long a nemesis for Feller. Fearlessly and confidently, Bobby hurled his fireball. The batter smashed a hard and wicked ground ball between first and second. The Cleveland second baseman barely knocked the ball down, pounced upon it, whirled quickly, and with all his might fired it to first base. It nipped the runner by a step, for the final out.

The game was over, and the crowd exploded with a thunderous roar to acclaim Bob Feller. Not only had he pitched his first no-hitter, but he had also hurled the first no-hit, no-run game on the Opening Day of a new major league season.

In the seventeen years that Bob Feller played in the big leagues, he went on to hurl two more no-hitters, pitched a record twelve one-hit games, set an all-time single season strikeout record of 348, fanned 2,538 batters while winning 262 major league games, and wound up immortalized in baseball's Hall of Fame. But to this day, Bobby's first no-hitter remains the only no-hit, no-run classic ever hurled on an Opening Day of a big league baseball season.

MARVELOUS MAMA

Down through the years, many remarkable women athletes have scaled the heights to everlasting sports fame. A flaxen-haired Dutch housewife and mother of two children, Fanny Blankers-Koen once performed a feat so incredible that it set her down in history as the greatest all-round female track and field athlete who ever lived.

Fanny began her pursuit of fame as a swimmer. But she was a flop. Unable to win races in the water, she went up on land and became an amazing performer on the cinders. She won an assortment of fifty European track and field championships.

In 1948, when the "Marvelous Mama" from Holland was thirty years old, she visited London, England, to compete in the Olympic Games. Although she held world records in the high jump and the broad jump, she had decided not to enter these events. Instead, she had decided merely to run.

She won the 100-meter sprint in 11.9 seconds. She won the 200-meter dash in 24.4 seconds. Then, she won the 80-meter hurdle race in 11.2 seconds for a world record. Thereby, she became the first female triple winner in the history of the Olympic Games.

But fabulous Fanny was not yet done. She ran the anchor leg to win the women's 400-meter relay race for her country. It completed the greatest track feat ever achieved by a woman. Fanny Blankers-Koen became the first and only woman in history to win four gold medals in one set of Olympic Games.

It is doubtful whether any other woman athlete will ever surpass or equal Fanny's record in the 1948 Olympics By winning four gold medals she gained immortality among the titans of the Olympic Games.

At twenty-nine, he reigned supreme as the pocket billiard champion of the world.

For almost three decades, he was the invincible master of one of the world's most difficult games. His success earned him the title of the Man With The Golden Arm.

Over the years, Willie the Wonder demolished the records of all the champions in the history of the game. He became the first player to run as many as 310 consecutive balls without a miss. Soon, he boosted that all-time record to 322, and then to 356.

But in March of 1954, at Springfield, Ohio, Mosconi stunned a sports world that had grown accustomed to his uncanny skill. On that day, he played 35 racks of pocket billiards without rest, and he ran off 525 consecutive balls without a miss.

MAN WITH
THE GOLDEN ARM

IT IS BELIEVED that pocket billiards, or pool, originated around the fourteenth century. Since then, untold millions of people all over the world have played the game for pleasure, fame or fortune. Unquestionably, the best player of all time was Willie Mosconi.

A native of Philadelphia, Willie was only five years old when he began climbing around a billiard table, wielding a cue stick twice as long as he was, to click the ivory balls. By the time he was seven, he was a prodigy who was being exhibited publicly in contests against all comers.

TWO TIMES A CHAMP

IN 1956, when Floyd Patterson was only twenty years and ten months old, he became the youngest prizefighter ever to gain the heavyweight title. This historic ring victory gloriously climaxed the strange story of a fighter who had to fight fear.

The son of a laborer and a humble domestic, Floyd was raised in the tenements of New York City. He was a shy and frightened boy who felt so insecure in the world around him that he became emotionally disturbed. At the age of ten, he could neither read nor write. To mask his feelings of insecurity he became a tough kid and a street fighter involved in petty crimes and acts of violence. Classified as a delinquent youth with a long truancy record, Floyd was committed to a correctional institution for wayward boys.

On his release a few years later, a great change was evident to all those who had known him. He had become a fine athlete, proficient in several sports. He was best at boxing and became so skilled an amateur boxer that in 1952 at seventeen, he gained international fame for his fistic prowess. At Helsinki, Finland, representing the United States, he won an Olympic gold medal by capturing the middleweight championship. Soon after, he embarked on a professional career in the ring.

Before he was twenty-one years old, he stunned the sports world by winning boxing's biggest and most coveted title. It was one of the most startling achievements in the annals of the sport.

After reigning as the world's heavyweight king for three years, Floyd Patterson defended his title against Ingemar Johansson of Sweden in a bout he was heavily favored to win. Instead, he took a cruel and humiliating beating and was knocked down seven times before the referee mercifully stopped the fight in the third round. The world had a new heavyweight champion.

Could he ever climb back to the top of the boxing world? Floyd Patterson knew that no heavyweight champion had ever come back to regain a lost title. He resolved to be the first to do it.

Finally the day came for the return bout between champion Johansson and ex-champion Floyd Patterson. This time the glamorous Swede went into the ring the strong favorite to win.

It was the night of June 20, 1960 when Floyd Patterson again met his conqueror. He had become a fighter with a mission. The opening bell had hardly sounded when Floyd threw two wicked punches to Johansson's face, implanting two red welts under his left eye. The ex-champion seemed supremely confident. In the second round Floyd ran into a murderous right that staggered him although he didn't go down. Instead he went after the champion more furuiously, lashing him with stinging jabs, doubling him up with left hooks and then coming in with hard rights to rock him. So it went until the fifth round when Patterson suddenly connected with a thundering left hook to the jaw that dropped champion Johansson to the canvas with a thud. He was up at nine. Floyd chased the foggy champion around the ring relentlessly. He finally cornered him and with cool precision dropped him for the sixth time with a flashing left hook to the jaw. Ingo crashed to the canvas. He did not move while the referee counted ten over him, and he was not to move under his own power until long after. Floyd leaped joyously into the air as the final count was reached. Once again Floyd Patterson was the heavyweight champion of the world. By his stunning victory he became the first heavyweight fighter of all time to regain the world's championship!

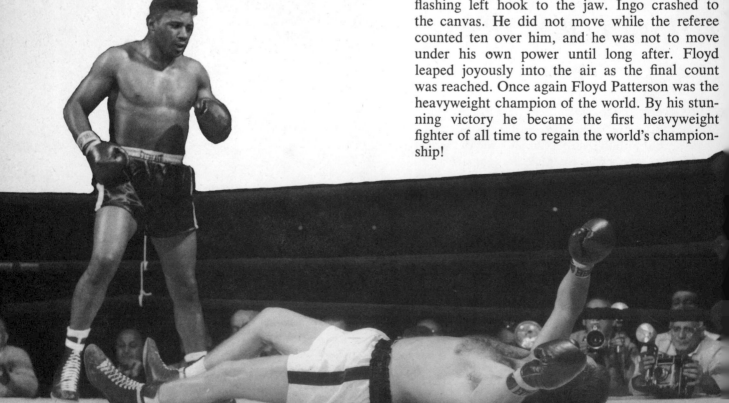

A THANKSGIVING FEAST

THE MOST UNBELIEVABLE individual scoring feat of big league professional football happened on November 28, 1929. On that Thanksgiving Day, in Chicago's snow-blanketed Comiskey Park, Ernie Nevers put on a one-man gridiron performance that never has been equaled.

One of the most versatile athletes of all time, Stanford's "Golden Boy" reached heroic proportions as a fullback in big time professional football. In 1929, when he was the player-coach of the Chicago Cardinals, Ernie Nevers not only played in all nineteen games his team engaged in that season, but even more, he played the full sixty minutes of every game.

On Thanksgiving Day of that year, before thousands of awed fans who gave up part of their holiday celebration to see him play, big, blond Ernie Nevers went on a scoring rampage that has never been matched.

The lowly Chicago Cardinals faced the famous Chicago Bears, featuring the immortal Red Grange. But player-manager Nevers was not impressed by the glamorous opposition. Aroused, he went on a wild spree that left the legendary Red Grange and his powerful teammates bewildered, shocked and crushed.

The game was only a few minutes old when fullback Nevers crashed through the enemy line for his first touchdown. Moments later, he scored another touchdown. By the time the half was over, he had three touchdowns.

However, his unquenchable thirst for competition drove him to play that contest to the hilt. In the second half, responding to the frenzied cheers of the crowd, Ernie Nevers continued to run wild, scoring three more touchdowns. At that game's end, he had six touchdowns and four conversions.

The lopsided score of 40-to-6 was a stunning victory for the Cardinals over the favored Bears. But what made that triumph unforgettable was the fact that Ernie Nevers had scored all forty points for his team. It was an all-time one-man and one-game scoring record for big time football.

A YEAR TO REMEMBER

BECAUSE OF A HAT, sport history gained a player who may very well have been the greatest golfer who ever lived.

When Byron Nelson was a poor and unknown boy caddying on a Ft. Worth golf course in Texas, the immortal Walter Hagen breezed into town to play in a tournament for the world's professional golf title.

It was a sun-drenched afternoon when the fabulous "Haig" found himself momentarily stymied on his way to capturing another golf championship. In that match there came a moment when he had to make a most difficult shot, but the blazing sun was blinding his vision. He needed something in a hurry to shade his eyes. So he turned to the gallery, spotted young Byron Nelson wearing a cap with a long sun visor, and he asked him for the loan of his hat. The awed youngster whipped off his cap and proudly offered it to the famous golf champ. Wearing Nelson's hat, Hagen went on to win the world's golf championship.

That incident set Byron Nelson's future. Then and there he determined to become a golf pro and emulate the feats of the great Walter Hagen. As he grew older, he gave up caddying and became a professional golfer. It was the beginning of an amazing saga.

Byron Nelson, who had learned to play as a poor caddy, became the most consistent hitter who ever played. He was the only golfer to finish "in the money" in 113 consecutive pro golf tournaments. That feat may never be matched.

In 1945, the amazing Byron Nelson recorded a year of golf triumphs which to this day seems fantastic. He accomplished the longest stretch of sustained winning golf any man had ever played. In thirty starts, he posted scores of 66 nineteen times.

Even more unbelievable, in that single year, always playing against the world's finest golfers, he won nineteen tournaments—twelve in a row. No one else has ever won as many major pro golf tournaments in one year, nor as many in a row. In achieving his fine record, he posted a per-round average of 69 for the whole year of 1945.

It is a record of golf greatness that may never be eclipsed.

A ROUND TRIP

WHEN ANTONIO ABERTONDO of Buenos Aires was eleven years old, he taught himself to swim. Since he lived only a few streets from the harbor where South America's La Plata River opens its mouth more than thirty miles wide, he spent most of his boyhood years in the water, developing into a skilled distance swimmer of amazing endurance. However, it wasn't until he was forty-two years old that he finally achieved the heroic swimming feat that stunned the world.

Ever since 1875, when England's Matthew Webb became the first man in history to swim across the English Channel, thousands of the world's most adventurous swimmers have tried to match his feat. But, scarcely more than one-hundred swimmers have succeeded in making this twenty-two-mile crossing from England to France.

Tony Abertondo became an old hand at conquering the Channel. Three times he swam from England to France to enhance his reputation as an outstanding distance swimmer. However, he still wasn't content. He had dedicated himself to a strange ambition: he resolved to become the first man ever to swim from England to France and back again. Most people laughed at him when he talked of a two-way Channel swim, for it always had seemed to be an impossible feat, beyond human endurance. But with assurance and stubborn single-mindedness Tony Abertondo prepared himself psychologically and physically for the attempt.

It was in the chilly dawn of a late September day in 1961 that the chunky Argentine swimmer, heavily greased for protection against the cold water, waded into the English Channel off the Dover coast and, with bold strokes, headed for France. Nearly nineteen hours later, he staggered ashore near Calais, having completed the first half of his two-way Channel swim. Quickly he gulped down a cup of hot coffee, then promptly plunged into the flood tide off Cap Gris Nez, this time to swim from France to England.

For many weary hours he battled the bewildering tides, as the angry Channel waves threatened to sweep him out to sea. He grew weak and as he neared the English coast he began to suffer from hallucinations. His fevered brain conjured up visions of gigantic fish swimming alongside him. The waves slapped his face into a swollen lump, and he could hardly see with his painfully sore eyes. But he refused to give up and continued stubbornly and fiercely to battle the icy waters, a lonely swimmer in a duel with the English Channel, whose treacherous currents have swept ships to their doom.

Finally, forty-three hours and five minutes after the start of his incredible two-way Channel swim, Tony Abertondo crawled out of the water and collapsed on an English beach. He had achieved a unique first, as the first man to swim from England to France and back again, in a single attempt. It was the most incredible feat in the history of swimming. More than that, it was one of the greatest triumphs of human endurance ever recorded.

TEN-GOAL TOMMY

POLO, ONE OF THE most ancient of sports, began in Persia where it was played before history was recorded. In time, it spread throughout the civilized world as a rich man's game.

Down through the years a host of men have achieved imperishable fame as polo titans. But no polo player ever captured the imagination of rich and poor alike as did Tommy Hitchcock, Jr., the prototype of the perfect American hero. As a polo performer he had to be seen to be believed. He was a sports hero truly out of the storybooks.

Born at the turn of the century with a golden spoon in his mouth, he learned to ride a horse almost as soon as he could walk. Although his father was a noted polo player, curiously it was his mother who began to teach him how to play polo when he was hardly thirteen. By the time he was sixteen, the blue-blooded rich boy was a rough, tough, slashing rider, and already an established star in polo.

He became a man early. When he was barely seventeen, he quit the game to fly and fight with France's famed Lafayette Escadrille, in the First World War. He served with distinction as a fighter pilot until his plane was shot down behind the enemy lines. After months in a prison camp, he made a daring escape by leaping through the window of a guarded train speeding across a river. Although he was wounded and relentlessly pursued, Tommy made his way on foot through enemy territory, over a distance of more than one hundred miles, to reach the safety of the neutral Swiss border.

After the war, when he returned to polo, he not only outclassed everyone to become the world's most glamorous and best player, but he also became the greatest horseman and the cleverest strategist as well as the hardest and longest hitter the game had ever known. His incredible feats with a polo pony and mallet revolutionized the game and imprinted his greatness upon the memories of millions of people. No player ever dominated the polo scene so completely and for so many years. Firebrand Tommy remained an unmatched polo-great for more than a quarter of a century. He became a living legend.

Death came to Tommy Hitchcock, Jr., at forty-four. During World War II when he was wearing the uniform of a United States Air Force lieutenant colonel, he was killed in a crash of a fighting plane.

It will be a long time before another Tommy Hitchcock turns up in polo. Only he in sports history ever achieved the unbelievable feat of winning a ranking of 10-goals (the absolute tops) over a span of eighteen years.

ALL ODDS
AGAINST HER

WILMA RUDOLPH was born into a poor family of nineteen children, but she was the unluckiest of them all. When she arrived in this world, she weighed hardly more than four pounds. Her survival was doubtful. When Wilma grew older, matters took a turn for the worse. Her childhood was a succession of diseases, double pneumonia, scarlet fever and a form of polio which paralyzed her legs. Between the ages of four and eight, crippled Wilma had to stay in bed.

However, a resolute mother decided that helpless Wilma was as deserving of normal health as the rest of her large brood. So each week, she wrapped Wilma in a blanket and took her ninety miles to the hospital. After years of medical treatment at the free clinic, plus countless hours of weary labor spent massaging the useless limbs, Wilma finally learned to walk, with a leg brace.

Her determination to be like other girls was no less than her mother's. At thirteen, Wilma was strong enough to run.

As she grew older, her running got her to Tennessee State University. There, the once crippled Wilma flowered into a graceful, fleet-footed, famous runner.

In 1960, Wilma was in Rome, Italy, to compete in the Olympic Games against the world's most fleet-footed women. She became the darling of the Olympics and a heroine for the whole world to know. Wonderful Wilma won the 100-meter sprint in eleven seconds. Then, she won the 200-meter race in twenty-four seconds. For good measure, she anchored the United States Olympic team to a victory and a world's record in the 400-meter relay.

It was the greatest track feat ever achieved by an American woman. By winning three gold medals, Wilma became the only track and field athlete, male or female, to emerge from the 1960 Olympic Games as a triple winner. Even more than that, she became the first American girl to capture as many as three gold medals in the Olympics.

As a triple Olympic winner Wilma Rudolph had her name inscribed in the record book as the greatest American female runner in sports history.

THE LITTLE NAPOLEON

However, later that season, the fabulous little general was to enrich his fame as a managerial genius. The "Little Napoleon" became displeased with his team, and he ripped it apart by discarding many of his players and trading away most of his stars—to field an almost completely new team for the finish of that pennant campaign.

On the 7th of September, the Giants opened their final home stand of the 1916 season. The fiery, jut-jawed McGraw led the charge to a new winning streak that was to stun the baseball world. Day after day, in single games or double-headers, his team continued to win, sweeping all the rival clubs of the National League.

The Giants' winning streak passed their earlier record of seventeen in a row, raced on to twenty, mounted to twenty-one and twenty-two, and still McGraw's team continued to win. Manager McGraw did the thinking for all his players, even to calling every pitch. Finally, on September 30, the Giants lost, and baseball's most remarkable winning streak came to an end. McGraw had led his players to twenty-six consecutive victories.

Neither of McGraw's two record winning streaks has been equalled in major league competition. Ironically, his greatest achievement was a bitter disappointment to him. Although he had piloted his players to seventeen victories in a row on the road and to twenty-six consecutive triumphs at home, his team finished the 1916 season in fourth place.

THEY NICKNAMED HIM the "Little Napoleon" of baseball, for he stood only sixty-six inches tall. In the thirty consecutive years that John J. McGraw was the swashbuckling manager of the New York Giants, he became a legend, immortalized as the greatest major league manager of all time. He piloted his team to ten pennants. No other manager topped this record.

As a wizard of the dugout, John McGraw piloted the Giants to the two most incredible winning streaks in the history of the major leagues. It happened in 1916.

In May of that baseball season, manager McGraw took his Giants on the road, and he astonished the baseball world by guiding his team through enemy territory to seventeen victories in a row. To this day, it stands as the all-time winning streak for a major league club playing away from home.

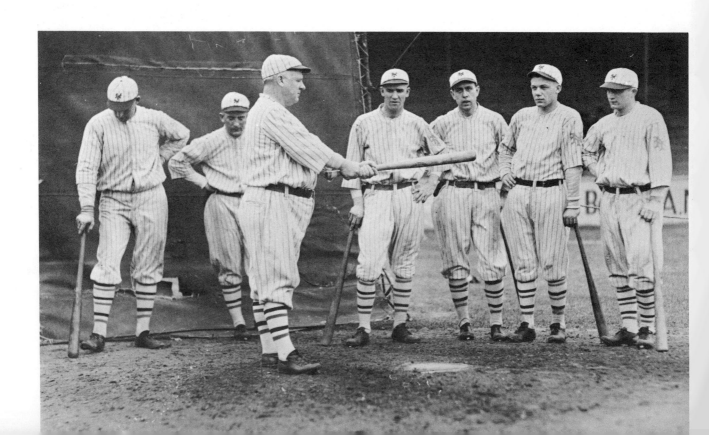

THE ESPO EXPRESS

IN THE 1944–45 National Hockey League campaign, the immortal Hall of Famer Richard (Rocket) Richard made imperishable hockey history by conquering an unreachable barrier. He became the first player ever to score fifty goals in a single season.

Twenty-four years later, the fabulous Bobby Hull eclipsed that historic feat by scoring fifty-four goals in one season.

But in their wildest dreams about their greatest seasons filled with wondrous feats, hockey stars could never have hoped to have such a glorious season as that produced by Phil Esposito for history as a scorer of goals, in the 1970–71 campaign.

A native of Sault Ste. Marie, Ontario, that sloe-eyed, gangly hockey center commanded scant attention as an outstanding scorer of goals during his first five years of playing for the Chicago Black Hawks. But no sooner was he traded to the Boston Bruins, a last-place team in the National Hockey League, he was surprisingly transformed into a phenomenal goal scorer.

In the 1970–71 season, "the Espo Express" as he came to be known and feared on the big league ice rinks, reached glory-heights never before attained by any other hockey great in history. He was unstoppable as he mowed down all tough opponents on his spectacular way to the all-time scoring record.

He scored one or more goals in thirty consecutive games. Seven times he accomplished the rare "hat trick" by scoring three goals in one game. He set a new all-time record for total points in one season—152. But his greatest achievement for his everlasting fame as hockey's incomparable goal scorer was the fantastic number of goals he scored in that one season, for the winning Boston Bruins. Never before has an all-time hockey record been eclipsed by a bigger margin. For in the 78 games Phil Esposito played, he scored an unbelievable total of 76 goals.

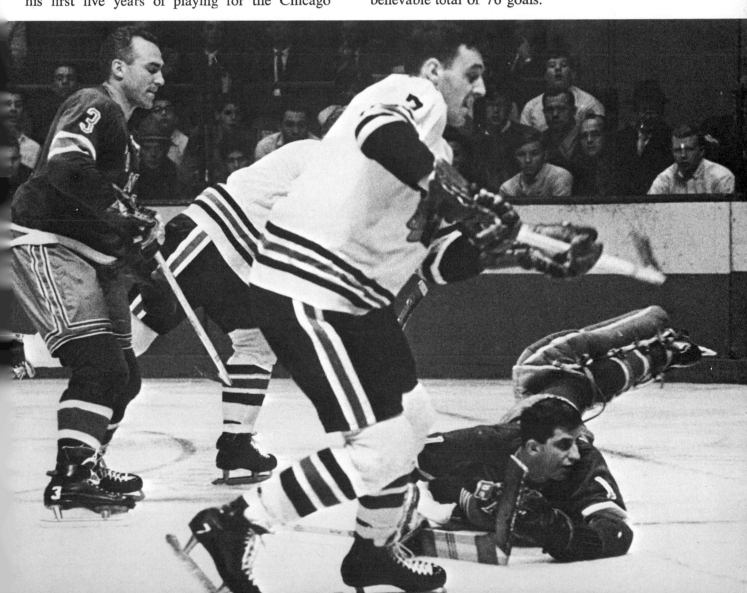

THE MAN WHO INCHED SKYWARD

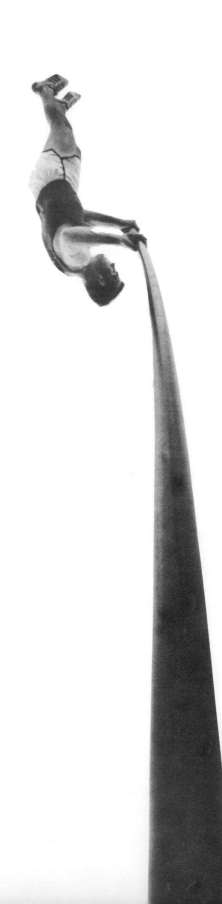

WHEN JOHN PENNEL — a well-rounded athlete who could broadjump better than twenty-three feet, run 100 yards in under ten seconds, and swim superbly—took up pole vaulting, he leaped for more than three years in total obscurity. Nevertheless, he was confident that a day would come when he would be at the top of the track world—hailed as the greatest pole vaulter of all. He was twenty-three when he finally began to tantalize the sports world with his pole vaulting.

On March 16, 1963, John Pennel leaped higher than he ever had before. Despite rain and wind marring that day, he sailed over a crossbar at a height of fifteen feet, nine inches. It was the beginning of an amazing saga of a man who inched skyward.

Five days later, competing in another track meet, and using a pole he had borrowed from a fellow competitor, he vaulted sixteen feet. Six times in 1963 he broke the world's pole vault record.

The sixth time he set a new pole vault mark was on August 24. It became an unforgettable day in sports history. In a track meet staged in his hometown of Miami, Florida, John Pennel flipped his 170-pound body over a crossbar set at 17 feet and ¾ inches.

Thus, he became the first man in history to pole vault 17 feet.

THE OLYMPIAN PRODIGY

NEVER BEFORE had a boy accomplished so much in world track and field competition at such an early age as Bob Mathias of Tulare, California. At the age of seventeen he won the grueling ten-event Olympic decathlon, the youngest athlete in history ever to do so. Even for the world's greatest athletes, the Olympic decathlon is the most demanding test of track and field skill and endurance ever devised. On two consecutive days, they must compete in the 100-meter dash, the broad jump, the high jump, the sixteen-pound shotput, the 400-meter run, the 110-meter high hurdles, the discus throw, the javelin throw, the pole vault and the 1,500-meter run. For schoolboy Bob Mathias, the 1948 Olympic Games in London were his first Olympiad. Surprisingly, before coming to England in quest of decathlon glory, he had never pole-vaulted, broad-jumped or held a javelin in his life; nor had he ever run the 400 or 1,500-meter races in competition.

Even more surprising was the fact that only three years earlier he had been a gangly, sickly youth who suffered from anemia and nosebleeds, and had to take iron and liver pills to build up his puny strength. Nonetheless, that curious seventeen-year-old came to compete against the world's greatest track and field stars from more than twenty nations.

Although the first day of the Olympic decathlon was gloomy and rainy, Bob Mathias gave a good account of himself in the 100-meter dash, the broad jump, the sixteen-pound shotput, the high jump and the 400-meter run. When that exhausting first day, which began at ten o'clock in the morning and lasted past eight at night, was over Bob stood in third place among the world's greatest decathlon athletes.

The next day, London's Empire Stadium was a sea of rain, mud and fog. It was the worst day in Olympic Games history. Dressed in a rain slicker and huddling under a blanket, Bob Mathias remained on the field for twelve hours, patiently waiting to compete in all the scheduled events. He had to pole vault with a pole too slippery to grip, he had to hurl the javelin when it was too dark to see the takeoff line, and when he was called to run the 1,500-meter race, it was already after ten o'clock at night. He finished that day fighting stomach cramps and completely worn out from his ordeal.

But he had won the Olympic decathlon, with an outstanding total of 7,139 points. Of all the world's greatest decathlon men who had competed in that Olympiad, schoolboy Bob was the only competitor to surpass the 7,000-point figure.

Four years later, Bob Mathias again won the Olympic decathlon—to become the first man in history to achieve an incredible double Olympic Games decathlon triumph.

THE GIBSON GIRL AGAINST THE WORLD

FOR ALTHEA GIBSON, the road to tennis fame was long and rocky.

Born on a poor cotton farm in South Carolina, she grew up in the ugly jungle slums of New York. Her girlhood home was the teeming streets of Harlem. By the time she was 12, Althea was a confirmed juvenile delinquent. She played hooky from school, ran wild with boy gangs, fought fist fights, and even drank liquor to show off her toughness. But she was an unusually talented natural athlete.

At 13, her sordid teenage life was changed by tennis. Presented with a second-hand racquet, she was persuaded to take up the game. Before long, she was outplaying grownups in local tournaments.

Although she played tennis ferociously, the Gibson girl found no road to fame. Her skin was black, and never before had anyone of her race played in major tennis tournaments.

However, in 1949, when Althea was 22, her skills with a racquet had grown so commanding and challenging that she broke down the color barrier in American tennis. She became the first Negro to compete in a national tennis tournament.

Although, the long-limbed 70-inch Gibson girl became a familiar figure on the big-time tennis circuit, her playing against the country's top women stars was disheartening. She lost more often than she won. Her struggle appeared hopeless. She became so discouraged that she wanted to give up the game .

Then in 1955, Althea was persuaded to embark on a tennis tour of Asia, as a good-will ambassador for her country. It was then that her playing began to blaze with surprising power. Her heart now back in tennis, she began to assert herself forcefully, as one of the world's great female players.

In 1957, although she was 30, an advanced age for a tennis player on the way up, Althea came to England to challenge the world's finest players for the famed Wimbledon crown, the symbol of tennis championship of the world. In an awesome display of powerful shot-making, she romped through that international tournament to become the first Negro in history to win the title. Humble Althea Gibson was received by Britain's Queen Elizabeth and presented with the most treasured trophy in tennis. Upon her return home, even the President of the United States acclaimed her feat.

However, Althea was not yet done with tennis fame. Before that glorious year had come to an end, she came to historic Forest Hills, where once again she outplayed the world's top distaff stars, and won the United States tennis championship. Again she made history, for she was the first of her race ever to capture an American national tennis title.

At long last, Althea Gibson became the greatest tennis player in the world. She was an unconquered queen with the tennis world truly at her feet. To prove that her pioneering victory had been no lucky fluke, on the following year the Gibson girl again captured the Wimbledon and American tennis titles, to continue her reign as the tennis champion of the world.

Her pioneering feat as a tennis champion made her unique in sports history.

A GRECIAN FLIGHT TO THE STARS

BORN IN THE town of Trikalla, Greece, Christos Papanicolaou never had pole vaulted until he was nineteen years old. Surprisingly and unwillingly, he became a pole vaulter. When he was a student at a Greek prep school, on the day of a track meet, he was handed a pole by the school's track coach who told him:

"We need someone to pole vault for our team. You're our vaulter!"

Vaulting for the first time in his life, Christos cleared eleven feet. A year later, he was vaulting over thirteen feet, and a year after that he was jumping higher than fifteen feet.

When Christos Papanicolaou came to the United States to study at San Jose State College, he was so fascinated with the skills and feats of America's most famous and greatest pole vaulters that he began to train and work hard to perfect his own technique as a pole vaulter. In the 1968 Olympic Games, he represented Greece in the pole vault event and he placed fourth.

Then, for almost two years thereafter, nothing was heard of Christos Papanicolaou as a pole vaulter. But finally there came a day in 1970 when the whole world suddenly heard of him as a pole vaulting wonder. For he achieved a feat which had been believed to be an impossible accomplishment for a track athlete.

On October 24th of that year, in an international track-and-field meet held in Athens, 28-year-old Christos Papanicolaou won the pole vault event with the most unbelievable leap ever made in sports history. He became the first man to pole vault over eighteen feet. His winning leap into the air had measured 18 feet plus ½ inch!

In the main square of the town of Trikalla, there now stands a statue of Christos Papanicolaou, to glorify the fame of an amazing Greek hero who had conquered an unreachable barrier.

THE UNWANTED CHAMPION

NO TWO-FISTED MAN ever emerged from a stranger or a more sordid background to attain ring fame than Charles "Sonny" Liston.

Born into a large family on a miserably shabby cotton farm in Arkansas, Sonny Liston in his dreary boyhood, knew little of home, love, guidance or schooling. He grew up a wild, brawling, illiterate youngster. At eighteen he was sentenced to prison as a thief.

When that truculent lad was shut away behind bars, a kindly prison chaplain taught him how to box. Hulking Sonny Liston was an apt pupil who became an athlete of some distinction. He won the heavyweight boxing championship of the Missouri State Penitentiary. It was the beginning of a strange ring saga.

Upon his release from prison, when Sonny Liston was twenty-one, he became a professional fighter. Huge, powerful, and with the largest fists in the ring, he compiled an astonishing victory record. Almost all of his bouts ended with a quick knockout.

But despite his growing fame, the sports world was reluctant to accept Sonny Liston as a fistic idol. He still snarled and sulked through life, and again and again, he ran afoul of the law. His police record became as familiar as was his ring record, and loud was the demand that he be outlawed from boxing.

Nevertheless, on the night of September 25, 1962, Sonny Liston climbed into a ring to face Floyd Patterson, the world's heavyweight champion, in a battle for pugilism's most coveted crown. On that memorable night, he made boxing history. He captured the heavyweight championship of the world in the quickest time recorded. He won in the first round by a knockout —in only 126 seconds!

Of all the ring-greats who punched their ways to the world's heavyweight title, none ever wrote his challenge across the skies with such awesome might and overwhelming brilliance as did Charles Sonny Liston.

FOR THE STANLEY CUP

SINCE 1893, the "world series" of hockey has been the annual play for the Stanley Cup, the symbol of the world professional hockey championship.

In 1938 the Chicago Black Hawks were coached by William Stewart, a major league baseball umpire. The club began the season as the weakest team in the National Hockey League. Most of its players were castoffs from other clubs. So futile were the Chicago Black Hawks of 1938 that in more than twenty weeks of big league competition, they won only fourteen games. But miraculously, they had sneaked into the Stanley Cup playoffs through the back door.

Once in the playoffs, the floundering Chicago Black Hawks caught fire. In the first round, playing spectacularly and with luck on their side, they eliminated the highly favored Montreal Canadians, perennial hockey champions. It caused a sensation.

In the next round, the now hopeful Chicago Black Hawks once again astonished the hockey-world by eliminating the powerful New York Americans, in a three-game series. The team which had won only fourteen games all season, now wound up playing in the "world series" of hockey. The Black Hawks now had to face the awesome Toronto Maple Leafs, then one of the greatest teams. A battle for possession of the legendary cup between the mighty Maple Leafs and mediocre Black Hawks, looked like a ludicrous mismatch.

On April 5, 1938, only a few hours before the start of the first game, in best-of-five-game series for the cup, the Hawks found themselves without a goal keeper; their regular goalie had been injured.

In a desperate search for a substitute goal keeper, the Hawks' manager found in a Toronto pub, a castoff minor-league goalie named Alfie Moore. Although he was woefully out of condition, and hadn't been on skates for years, he was hired to play for the Chicago club. They eased him under a cold shower and forced him to drink hot black coffee to get him ready to play that night.

In the first game, goalie Alfie Moore was a sensation. He made so many saves that he sparked the Hawks to a victory.

Nothing could stop the Chicagoans now. They swept the next two games and wound up in possession of the Stanley Cup.

A LONG WAIT FOR VICTORY

NO ONE FIGURED Jack Westland for a winner. At 47 he was too old to stand a chance of winning the 1952 National Amateur Golf Championship. His opponent was a young, skilled tournament golfer, Al Mengert. Yet there was Westland in the finals of the tourney, and if he won he would become the oldest man ever to triumph in this much sought-after amateur golf title.

The contrast between Mengert and Westland was even greater than their ages indicated. Mengert was a golfer of such consistent quality that he had served as an alternate on the Unite States Walker Cup team. On the other hand, Westland had been busy campaigning for a seat in the United States House of Representatives. Only a hasty rearranging of his schedule allowed him to compete in the tournament.

Westland's appearance in the National was his first participation since 1947. His tries for the title were infrequent. Mengert, of course, was active on the tournament trail and seemed a sure thing to overpower his older opponent. After all, no player Westland's age had ever won the title.

When Westland managed to survive the elimination rounds of the tournament, the familiar story of the 1931 finals was told again. At that time, when Mengert was only two years old, Westland was a twenty-six year old playing against famed Francis Ouimet. It had been a disaster for Westland. Inexperienced, he was badly defeated by Ouimet. After that match, Westland had faded back into the ranks, just another competent golfer.

Now once more Westland was in the final round. But again it seemed that he was not destined to win. At forty-seven, he was deemed too old to have a chance.

Both golfers were at the top of their games. Drives split the fairways. Approach shots were crisp and accurate. Surprisingly, Westland took the lead. The principal reason was his hot putter. He was brilliant on the greens, and by the eighteenth hole, he led Mengert by one hole.

Tension increased as the crowd wondered if thirty-six holes in one day would be too tough a grind for the veteran. After the twenty-seventh hole, Mengert took the lead. The experts agreed that this was the time that Westland would surely fold under the continuous pressure applied by his young foe.

But Westland was not through. Grimly, he hung on, fighting to realize a dream that had stayed with him for twenty-one years. He evened the match on the next hole. And on the thirtieth hole, he took the lead. He also won the thirty-second hole. The momentum had shifted in Westland's favor. Then, on the thirty-fourth hole, it was all over. A par clinched the title for Westland. The gallery broke its silence with an approving cheer. For once, at least, the calendar had been shunted aside to let a veteran have his place in the sun.

After a twenty-one year wait, Jack Westland had become the National Amateur Champion, the oldest player ever to win this most coveted of all amateur golf titles. It was a golfing achievement that may never be duplicated again!

FIVE FANNED THE BREEZE

THE ALL-STAR GAME, the annual "dream game" of the two major leagues, was in 1934 truly a baseball fan's dream come true. The diamond stars playing in the classic that year for both the National League and the American League composed the most glamorous line-ups ever presented for a baseball game. Eighteen of the athletes who competed in the 1934 All-Star Game are now among the immortals enshrined in baseball's Hall of Fame. But it was Carl Hubbell, the screwball-throwing lefty, who emerged from that July 10 classic as the most unforgettable All-Star hero. It was because southpaw Hubbell struck out five men in a row.

The tall, gangling lefty had been selected to open for the National League stars. His assignment was to stop the mightiest collection of sluggers ever assembled to play on one baseball team. Within only a few moments of the umpire's cry of "Play ball" Hubbell appeared inadequate to the task. Second-baseman Charley Gehringer, the legendary "mechanical man" of baseball history, led off with a single and went to second on an error. Then, surprisingly, control artist Hubbell walked the next batter. Up to bat came the immortal Babe Ruth, the greatest home run slugger of all time. Fearlessly, "King Carl" faced the mighty "King of Swat" who had by that time 714 home runs to his credit, and struck him out on four pitched balls.

That brought to bat Lou Gehrig, the murderous slugger with 494 home runs to his credit. Hubbell was not fazed. He struck Gehrig out with four pitches.

Then it was Jimmy Foxx who came to bat, the second greatest home run hitter of all time, with 534 four-baggers at that time. Still, southpaw Hubbell wasn't bothered. He used only three screwballs to strike out the menacing Foxx.

The fans went wild acclaiming Hubbell's talents. But he had not yet finished his pitching masterpiece! To start the second inning, he had to face Al Simmons, a fearsome home run slugger who was in his eleventh consecutive .300 season. Hubbell struck out Simmons. The next batter, Joe Cronin, was recognized as the greatest clutch hitter in baseball history. Cronin went down swinging, also a strikeout victim.

Even to the thousands of fans who saw it happen, that sequence seemed impossible. Carl Hubbel had faced five of the most feared and greatest sluggers in the annals of the national pastime, and he had struck out all five in a row.

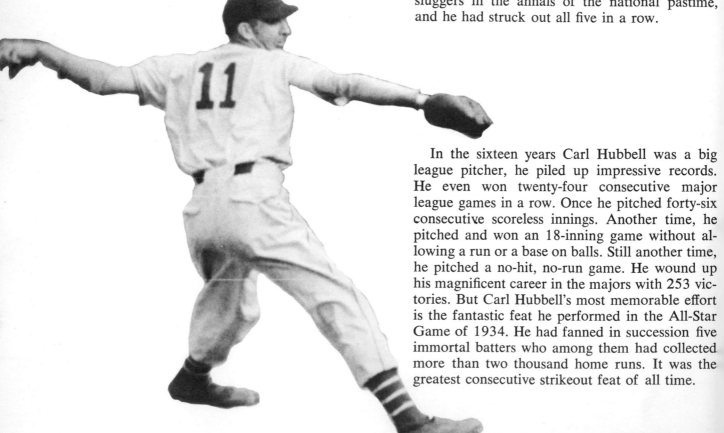

In the sixteen years Carl Hubbell was a big league pitcher, he piled up impressive records. He even won twenty-four consecutive major league games in a row. Once he pitched forty-six consecutive scoreless innings. Another time, he pitched and won an 18-inning game without allowing a run or a base on balls. Still another time, he pitched a no-hit, no-run game. He wound up his magnificent career in the majors with 253 victories. But Carl Hubbell's most memorable effort is the fantastic feat he performed in the All-Star Game of 1934. He had fanned in succession five immortal batters who among them had collected more than two thousand home runs. It was the greatest consecutive strikeout feat of all time.

THE FASTEST HUMAN

IN TRACK MEETS, the man who has held the world record for the 100-yard dash has traditionally been acclaimed "the world's fastest human."

In 1961, this coveted title was captured by twenty-one-year-old Frank Budd, who had almost no encouragement from nature. He was a runner with a distinct handicap—one leg weaker than the other.

Frank Budd of Asbury Park, New Jersey, became a sprinter most reluctantly. As a schoolboy he happily starred in football and basketball. His father, a one-time track star, constantly urged Frank to concentrate on running. Merely to please his father, Frank ran when there was nothing more exciting for him to do.

When he became a student at Villonova College, still prodded by his father, Frank went out for the track team. He hardly impressed the school's track coach as a future great. He ran with a pronounced limp. His right leg was smaller at the calf and thigh and weaker than his left. It was the result of a childhood illness that might have been polio.

The coach prescribed a unique method of training to correct Budd's limping condition. Frank did weight-lifting, and he ran up and down the seats of the athletic stadium wearing a ten-pound vest.

Before long, surprisingly, Frank became one of the nation's best sprinters.

On June 24, 1961 he competed at Randalls Island Stadium in New York City in the National A.A.U. championship track meet, and challenged the country's fastest runners for the 100-yard national title. There had been showers that morning, leaving the track slightly wet and a trifle heavy.

In the finals of the 100-yard dash, Frank Budd faced three famous sprinters who all had equaled the world record of 9.3 seconds for the distance. That record had stood for so many years that the track world had come to believe that 9.3 seconds was the limit of man's speed in running 100 yards.

The brilliant field of six runners awaited the starter's signal. Twice there were false starts, and the tension mounted. Suddenly, the starter's gun barked, and the six runners surged forward in a clean break. Although Frank Budd had none of the best at the start of the race, in a few twinkling seconds his fast legs inched him to the front. With each stride he ran faster than he had ever run before, and stubbornly he held on to his slim lead. With less than twenty yards more to go, the six sprinters were running virtually even. As they neared the finish line, Frank Budd generated an extra burst of speed and came home in first place.

Moments later, the announcer's voice stilled the roar of the crowd, and it boomed throughout the arena: "The winner of the 100-yard dash, number twenty-five, Frank Budd of Villonova College. His time—a new world record of 9.2 seconds!"

It was the fastest 100 yards ever run by a human.

THE LONGEST DAY FOR A FOOTBALL COACH

AMOS ALONZO STAGG's football coaching record staggers the imagination.

Son of a humble shoemaker, Stagg had planned to dedicate his life to the clergy. He turned from the pulpit when, at Yale University, he gained national fame as one of the greatest football players of all time.

In 1890, he became a football coach in Massachusetts at tiny Y.M.C.A. Springfield College, famed as the birthplace of the game of basketball. Two years later, when Chicago University first opened its doors, Stagg became its football coach.

There, he became famous as the most inventive of all football coaches. He molded many championship teams and developed a host of immortal players. He remained Chicago's football coach for an astonishing span of forty-one consecutive years.

When he was seventy, he was urged to retire as head football coach. Indignantly, he refused, and he went off to another college to coach its football teams. There, he continued as a football coach for another decade. When he was eighty-one years old, he was still so potent as a gridiron mentor that he was acclaimed the outstanding college football coach.

However, once again he was urged to retire from coaching because of his age. Again Stagg refused, and he went off to coach still another college football team. He continued as a college football coach until he was almost ninety-eight years old. When he finally quit, it ended the longest career a football coach ever had. Amos Alonzo Stagg was a college football coach for seventy straight years!

thrower, and hurdler. She won more than 1,100 major track and field contests, and she set approximately one hundred different world and national records.

When Stella Walsh was in her 40's, she amazed the sports world as a Pentathlon performer. From 1950 through 1954, she won the grueling five-event United States Pentathlon championship five consecutive times. No other woman has matched her for track versatility.

In 1963, although she was fifty-two years old, Stella was still competing against the best of her sex.

The ageless Stella Walsh must stand out as the most durable woman athlete of all time.

THE AGELESS WOMAN

THE WORLD first heard of Stella Walasiewicz of Poland as a runner when she won the 100 meter championship in the 1932 Olympic Games. It was the beginning of the longest athletic saga ever created by a woman.

Soon after her Olympic victory she settled in the United States, changed her name to Stella Walsh, and embarked on a track career without parallel in sports history.

Over the years, she not only ran foot races from sixty yards to the mile, but she also competed against the world's top female athletes as broad jumper, high jumper, shot putter, discus

HIS LAST AUTOMOBILE RIDE

AUTO RACING DRIVER Juan Manuel Fangio of Argentina was determined to perform the impossible and show the world that his fabled supremacy at the wheel was no myth.

The small, greying world driving champion was forty-six when on August 4, 1957, he climbed into his Maserati car to race in Germany's Grand Prix, the toughest and most dangerous auto race in the world. The treacherous Nürburgring course in the Eifel Mountains had taken many lives in payment for racing fame and fortune.

It was Fangio's last race. He had given many years of his life to auto racing all over the world, and now at long last he had decided to retire.

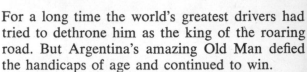

For a long time the world's greatest drivers had tried to dethrone him as the king of the roaring road. But Argentina's amazing Old Man defied the handicaps of age and continued to win.

Now, Germany's Grand Prix was to be his farewell race to glory. From the start Fangio drove as he never had before. Over the curving roads of Nürburgring which climbed to dizzy heights, the cool Old Man in his Maserati skidded around the hairpin turns like a wild young madman.

But other drivers stuck with him and it was a fight to the finish. When Fangio got the winner's checkered flag, he was only three seconds ahead of his nearest rival. He had covered the 312.4 miles in the astonishing time of 30 minutes, 38.3 seconds.

It was a great race, but for Juan Fangio it was more than that. It sealed his glory as a racing immortal for the ages. With that victory the forty-six year old Argentine daredevil achieved a record that is unlikely ever to be equaled. He had captured the auto driving championship of the world—for an unprecedented fifth year in succession.

[116]

HEAVY WAS HIS LOAD

FROM EARLIEST TIME, man out of necessity has been a weight lifter. But the Europeans were the first to make a sport out of weight lifting. However, the man whose accomplishments were most spectacular in the muscular game of raising weights was the American, Paul Anderson.

The 304-pound strong man from Toccoa, Georgia, first gained universal fame for his prowess in 1956 when he won the world's weight lifting championship at the Olympic Games in Australia. But not too long after, that Olympic champion performed a weight lifting feat, before his hometown admirers, which left the world gaping in disbelief. On June 12, 1957 he raised the greatest weight ever lifted by a human.

In a herculean back lift, he raised a weight of 6,000 pounds.

The closest any strong man ever came to matching Anderson's superhuman achievement was in 1896 when the fabulous Canadian weight lifter, Louis Cyr, set a world's record by lifting 4,133 pounds.

But Paul Anderson's lift of three tons was the most incredible feat ever credited to a human being in the sport of weight lifting.

A TRIGGER MAN FOR THE AGES

SINCE THE INVENTION of the gun, millions of people the world over have aimed and fired guns at various targets. But no other man ever fired a gun with greater endurance and more amazing skill than Adolph Topperwein. To gain fame as the best marksman the world has ever known, he once achieved a shooting feat that has never been equalled.

Born in San Antonio, Texas in 1869, Topperwein, son of a gunsmith, learned to shoot a rifle at a tender age. Before he was eleven, he was already bragging to his patch-pants friends that he would grow up to become the world's greatest marksman.

When the boy grew older, he became a star performer in the circus and on vaudeville stages, giving shooting exhibitions with rifle, handgun and shotgun that won him world fame as a trick-shot marksman. For years, he toured, giving such amazing demonstrations of marksmanship that his name became a household word. At one time, he held fourteen world records for shooting at set-up and moving targets.

In 1907, when Adolph Topperwein was thirty-eight years old, he undertook to set a new shooting record. For amazing skill and iron endurance, it was to be a feat that would shatter all previous records. The gritty Texan announced that he would attempt to fire a .22 caliber rifle for eight straight hours a day, on ten consecutive days. The targets at which he would shoot were two and one-fourth inch thick wooden blocks, thrown about thirty feet into the air and twenty-five feet in front of his firing line. He was to fire at his targets about every five seconds, an average of more than a thousand times an hour.

On the morning of December 13, 1907, a skeptical crowd gathered at the San Antonio fairgrounds to watch the start of Ad Topperwein's shooting marathon. Three officials—a referee, a judge and a scorekeeper—were to supervise and to attest to the accuracy of the figures.

For eight consecutive hours, Ad Topperwein aimed a five and one-fourth pound rifle at 7,500 small wooden cubes tossed high in the air, and he did not miss once. Rifles were changed after every 500 shots because of overheated barrels.

On the second day, he fired at 7,000 tiny flying wooden blocks and only once missed hitting his target. On the third day, he fired at 7,500 more wooden cubes and missed none.

On the fourth straight day, the marathon became a physical ordeal for Ad Topperwein. At the firing line he was in constant misery; his arms and shoulders ached from holding his rifle aloft. But his aim was almost perfect: out of 7,000 targets he missed only two. As he toed the firing line the next day he realized that his neck muscles were extremely painful and his vision blurred. His friends pleaded with him to quit, but he was determined to continue as long as he could raise a rifle to his shoulder and squeeze the trigger. On his fifth consecutive day at the firing line, he aimed at 8,000 targets and missed none! The following day he shot at 7,000 targets and missed once. But on the seventh day, he fired at 7,000 more wooden cubes and his score was again perfect.

The eighth day at the firing line was his worst. He was so weary that the targets seemed hopelessly blurred, but he continued firing at the flying wooden blocks, missing only four times out of 7,000. The ninth consecutive day, he recovered his incredible accuracy and blasted away at 8,000 more targets, missing none. On the tenth and final day of his fantastic marathon, Ad Topperwein couldn't lower his arms below the waist and he had to be helped to the firing line. But he aimed at 6,500 targets and missed only once.

When he had fired his last shot, Topperwein was so utterly exhausted by the ordeal that he collapsed and had to be carried off on a stretcher.

Ad Topperwein had achieved a feat of outstanding marksmanship. For eight hours a day, on ten consecutive days, he had fired a rifle at flying targets—tiny wooden cubes thrown high into the air—and out of 72,500 targets aimed at, he had missed only nine times!

THE FEMALE ROBIN HOOD

NO ONE IS CERTAIN just how far back into antiquity archery extends. But of all the sports played today, it is the oldest. As early as the fifth century, archery developed as an organized sport. Once the skill to shoot with a bow and arrow was necessary for hunting, warfare and self-preservation. But now, archery is a competitive sport for millions of people throughout the world.

Over the years, a host of archery champions have performed astonishing feats to carve their fame into sports history, and Nancy Vonderheide of Cincinnati, Ohio is among the most amazing.

It was only by accident that she became an archer. Unlike most athletes in pursuit of sports fame, she did not grow up on playing fields. Nevertheless, once she took up the game of bows and arrows, to escape boredom on dull Sunday afternoons, she wasted no time to become the most remarkable world champion in the history of archery. Even more amazing, she started her march to glory at the top of the archery world.

Even though she had not yet won a single minor archery contest, in 1961 that unknown American girl went to Oslo, Norway, to compete in the most important international bow and arrow tournament in the sport. It was for the archery championship of the world. In that contest for world supremacy, the most skilled female archers from all over the globe had to shoot seventy-two arrows a day, at distances from thirty to seventy meters, for four consecutive days. For Nancy, it was her first major archery tournament. Nevertheless, she not only captured the archery championship of the world, but in winning her first title, she set two world records.

Now that Nancy Vonderheide was the new archery champion of the world, she set out to enlarge her image and enrich her fame as a female Robin Hood. She embarked on an amazing streak of consecutive triumphs never before equaled. Through two unprecedented years, she captured every important bow and arrow title in sight. She won sixteen major archery tournaments in a row. It was an unbelievable feat of archery greatness unmatched in the history of the world's oldest sport.

HIS SHOES WERE NOT FOR WALKING

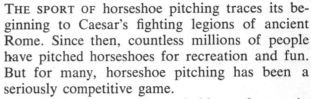

THE SPORT OF horseshoe pitching traces its beginning to Caesar's fighting legions of ancient Rome. Since then, countless millions of people have pitched horseshoes for recreation and fun. But for many, horseshoe pitching has been a seriously competitive game.

Probably the most remarkable performer in the history of this sport was a stubby little man from Boulder, Colorado named Ted Allen. Seven times he reigned as the horseshoe pitching champion of the world. Some of the phenomenal feats he accomplished have never been topped.

In the thirties and forties Ted Allen traveled annually about 50,000 miles to pitch horseshoes against all comers. Often, to display his astonishing skill he exhibited in a spectacular horseshoe pitching act in which he lighted matches with his steel shoes, knocked cigars from the mouths of human targets, and pitched ringers from the back of a horse.

Several times in professional competition for big stakes Ted Allen tossed ninety-eight consecutive ringers. Once, in a qualifying round of a national championship tournament, he set an unbelievable world record by tossing 180 ringers out of 200 throws.

However, his most incredible feat took place on August 25, 1941, at Des Moines, Iowa. The occasion was a tournament for the United States championship.

In the final round for the title, his opponent was Guy Zimmerman, one of the world's greatest in the pitching art. For eighty-two innings of play, each man matched the other, pitch for pitch and ringer for ringer. Each threw 164 shoes, and each dropped 145 of them cleanly around the stake. In sixty-five innings, Zimmerman scored ringers with both shoes, sixty-four times. It was a fantastic display of precision and skill in the art of pitching horseshoes. Yet, Ted Allen topped it. For in his sixty-five innings, he scored ringers with both shoes sixty-five times.

In winning the most remarkable match ever played, Ted Allen recorded the greatest performance in the history of horseshoe pitching.

ON A TIGHTROPE TO NOWHERE

NIAGARA FALLS, one of the world's most popular honeymoon spots, always has had an irresistible lure for hardy swimmers and daredevil screwballs. Once, defying death at Niagara Falls was a popular sport that attracted tremendous crowds. Of all the tightrope walkers who gambled with life at Niagara Falls, only one actually won universal fame and fortune. He was Emile Blondin, an athlete from France.

In the summer of 1859 Blondin came to the famed Niagara Falls, announcing that he would cross it on a tightrope stretched 200 feet above the roaring waters. It became the most talked-about sports event in the United States and Canada. On the appointed day a crowd of about a million spectators turned out to see the daring Frenchman take the fateful walk. Among the vast crowd of spectators watching from the Canadian and American shores were the President of the United States, the Prince of Wales, governors from many states, millionaires, socialites and gamblers. Fortunes were wagered on the outcome of Blondin's walk across Niagara Falls, and the optimists were justified in their faith, for he crossed Niagara Falls in only five minutes!

That balancing act catapulted him to world fame. He made a fortune appearing on the stage in the United States, Canada and Europe.

However, Emile Blondin was not fully satisfied with his spectacular conquest of Niagara Falls. He announced that once more he would walk across Niagara Falls — but this time, the hard way! He would walk across carrying a man on his back. A man named Harry Colcord volunteered to do it. Again, almost a million spectators turned out to watch him.

On a tightrope stretched 200 feet above Niagara Falls, the amazing Emile Blondin, carrying a man on his back, began his fantastic walk. When he was 100 feet out, Blondin stopped for a rest and ordered the man on his back to climb down for a moment. The frightened man dismounted and stood shivering on the tightrope, frantically clinging to Blondin's hips so as not to fall to his death.

After a minute's pause he climbed back, and Blondin began to run along the tightrope to the safety station. He made it! Cheering men acclaimed him the world's most daring athlete! As for Harry Colcord, the man who had crossed Niagara Falls on Blondin's back, the experience had been so frightening that he remained a mental case for the rest of his life.

But Blondin reaped his greatest reward after the second conquest of Niagara Falls. Wherever he appeared throughout the world, people went wild over him! Everybody wanted to see the man who had defied death at Niagara Falls by performing the strangest sports feat ever attempted by an athlete in quest of fame.

[M. BLONDIN CROSSING THE RIVER NIAGARA ON A TIGHT-ROPE.]

THE CHAMPION
OF CHAMPIONS

ONE OF THE world's oldest sports has been the game of batting a ball by hand against a wall. The early name of the game was "Fives" — five fingers to the hand. However, handball in its modern form (one-wall or four-wall) began as a game in Ireland in the eleventh century. Its popularity grew and spread throughout all Europe. In the 1840s, the game was brought to the United States when several of Ireland's best players migrated to America.

Curiously, Joe Platak of Chicago, Illinois, eventually achieved universal fame as the greatest handball player in history, by reason of the unprecedented feats he accomplished between 1935 through 1945. For eleven years, although he always played against the world's outstanding handball marvels, he rarely lost a contest.

He developed into such a wizard in the art of hitting a ball by hand against a wall that only he ever captured the handball championship of the world nine times.

That record immortalized Joe Platak in sports history as the champion of all handball champions.

[123]

21-4-59
2,664 LBS
A DEAN
CEDUNA

THE FISH THAT DIDN'T GET AWAY

FISHERMEN THE world over have been known to be whopping fibbers when boasting of their catches. But Alf Dean of Mildura, Australia, once achieved a fishing feat he truthfully could boast of, even though it was almost beyond belief.

On April 21, 1959 when he sailed out in his boat for some deep sea fishing at Denis Bay, near Cedura, South Australia, he hoped for a good catch. He was a noted big game fisherman who over the years had gained fame for his unusual exploits. But before that memorable day was over, even he was surprised by his astonishing accomplishment. It made fishing history.

He hooked the most fantastic monster ever caught by a fisherman. After a long and fierce battle between man and fish, he finally ended that grueling tug of war by landing his catch. It was a sixteen-foot ten-inch long man-eating white shark.

Alf Dean's incredible catch set an all-time all-tackle world record. It was the biggest fish ever caught with a rod and reel anywhere in the world. When it was officially ratified, the fish caught by Alf Dean weighed 2,664 pounds.

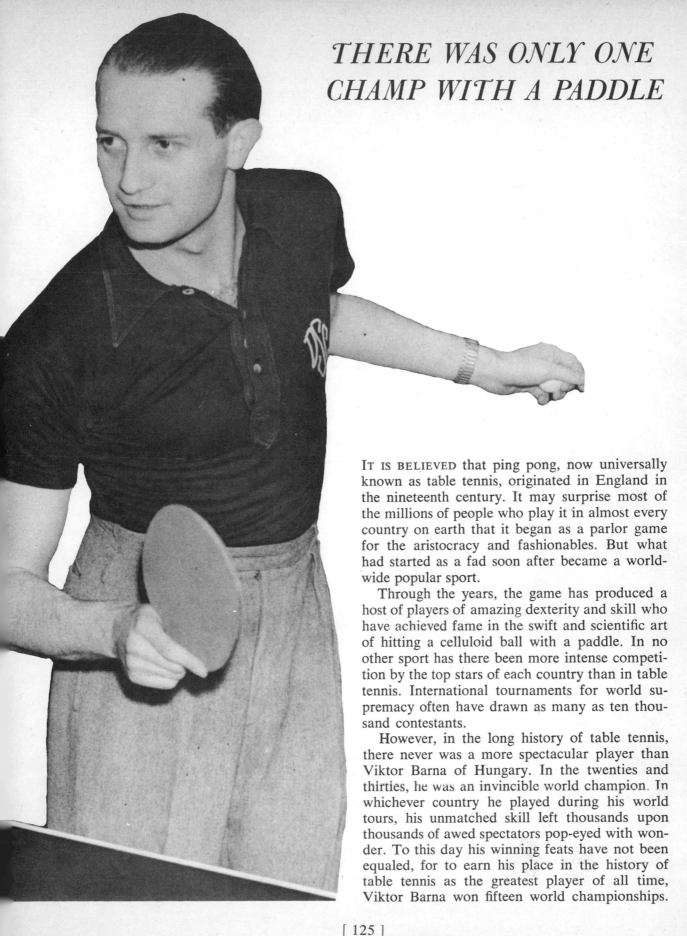

THERE WAS ONLY ONE CHAMP WITH A PADDLE

IT IS BELIEVED that ping pong, now universally known as table tennis, originated in England in the nineteenth century. It may surprise most of the millions of people who play it in almost every country on earth that it began as a parlor game for the aristocracy and fashionables. But what had started as a fad soon after became a world-wide popular sport.

Through the years, the game has produced a host of players of amazing dexterity and skill who have achieved fame in the swift and scientific art of hitting a celluloid ball with a paddle. In no other sport has there been more intense competition by the top stars of each country than in table tennis. International tournaments for world supremacy often have drawn as many as ten thousand contestants.

However, in the long history of table tennis, there never was a more spectacular player than Viktor Barna of Hungary. In the twenties and thirties, he was an invincible world champion. In whichever country he played during his world tours, his unmatched skill left thousands upon thousands of awed spectators pop-eyed with wonder. To this day his winning feats have not been equaled, for to earn his place in the history of table tennis as the greatest player of all time, Viktor Barna won fifteen world championships.

STRIKEOUTS BY SANDY

SANDY KOUFAX was only eighteen when he came off the Brooklyn sandlots to pitch in the big leagues. With his first victory in the majors, on August 27, 1955, he staked his claim to fame as a strikeout wonder. He fanned fourteen men in hurling a two-hit shutout.

As the seasons went by, southpaw Sandy gained unique distinction as a hurler for strikeouts. In over a thousand innings he pitched in the majors, he whiffed at least one batter for each frame. No other pitcher in the history of baseball ever averaged a strikeout an inning.

In time, this left-handed wonder achieved three strikeout feats beyond compare.

The first happened on the night of August 31, 1959. Before 82,794 frenzied onlookers, pitching against the San Francisco Giants, Sandy struck out eighteen men in nine innings. He was the first hurler in history to fan that many batters in a major league game played at night.

The second display of skill was accomplished in broad daylight, on April 24, 1962. Facing the Chicago Cubs, once more he struck out eighteen men in nine innings. Thus, he became the only pitcher in history to whiff eighteen batters in nine innings — twice.

In October of 1963, Sandy performed his third unparalleled strikeout feat. Pitching against the mighty New York Yankees in the World Series, he sparked the Los Angeles Dodgers to the baseball championship of the world, by setting an astonishing strikeout record. In the two games he won, he fanned twenty-three men.

In 1966, when Sandy Koufax suddenly quit the majors forever, because of a painful arthritic pitching arm, he left behind him an awesome record for his Hall of Fame immortality. Winner of 165 games, he enriched them with hurling feats beyond compare. Only he ever struck out 382 batters in one season, fanned 2,396 men in 2,324 innings, and hurled four no-hit-no-run games. He wrote his challenge across the baseball skies, perhaps for as long as big league baseball lives.

HE PUT A NATION
ON SKIS

TORGER TOKLE never achieved the glory of becoming the greatest ski jumper of all time. But he lived to become the most famous ski performer America has ever known. He accomplished a unique feat in the history of skiing. Only he ever put a nation on skis.

He was a nineteen year old schoolboy when in the winter of 1939, he arrived in the United States, an unknown immigrant from Norway. Since childhood, he had been leaping off icy slopes. He had been only six when he had negotiated his first ski jump.

Less than twenty-four hours after Torger Tokle had disembarked in the country, he was on a snow-blanketed hill competing in a ski-jumping meet. Although, he was wearing borrowed skis, he won the contest. His best jump on his first day in America was 152 feet.

For the husky youngster from Norway, it was an impressive beginning. He wasted little time to achieve fame as the most popular ski performer ever seen in the United States. In his first year in the strange land, he won fifteen ski meets and set nine records.

As time went by he jumped in every state where there was snow, and he was never outdistanced. After winning thirty-six ski meets, he was acclaimed America's ski king.

His record leaps through the frozen air were awesome. In 1941, he set a new American mark with an astonishing jump of 273 feet. Shortly after, he topped it with an amazing leap of 288 feet.

On March 1, 1942, at Iron Mountain, Michigan, he performed his greatest jump to glory. On that day, the Pine Mountain slide, famed as one of the largest in the world, was icy hard, and not in perfect condition for record jumping. Nevertheless, on his first leap, Torger Tokle soared into the air for 281 feet. It was a new record for that ski chute. But he came down with such force against the side of the hill that he cracked one of his skis.

He had no time to replace his damaged ski, nor borrow another, before attempting his second jump. He climbed back on the trestle, and fearlessly pushed off for his glide down the treacherous slide. With baited breath, more than 25,000 spectators watched his flight. When he descended to earth, history was made. For he had set a new American record with a fantastic jump of 289 feet.

No one else did as much to popularize the sport of skiing in America as Torger Tokle did with his spectacular jumping feats. He made all America ski conscious. Because of him, millions of Americans took up the sport.

Perhaps Torger Tokle might have become the greatest skier in history, if in 1942, he had not answered the call of duty for World War II.

On March 3, 1945, while leading an American ski patrol in combat, over the rugged snow-blanketed mountains in Italy, he was killed by an enemy shell. He was only twenty-five years old when he gave his life for his adopted country—the nation he had put on skis.